The Disciple Whom Jesus Loved

Take another look

The Bible has the answer

J. Phillips

Free printable copies of this Bible study are available at
www.TheDiscipleWhomJesusLoved.com

The Disciple Whom Jesus Loved
© 2011 by J. Phillips, Fifth Edition (First Edition © 2000)

Free printable Bible study version online at:
www.TheDiscipleWhomJesusLoved.com
Tags: Gospel of John authorship, beloved disciple, fourth gospel

Send all correspondence to:
TheDiscipleWhomJesusLoved.com
PO Box 885, Lockport, IL 60441
Phone: (770) 842-6370

ISBN13: 978-0-9702687-3-0
Library of Congress Control Number: 2011927685

Printed in the United States by:
Waymaker Communications
6774 Oak Ridge Commerce Way
Austell, GA 30168
(678) 838-6991

Dedication

Thank you, God, for the question that was raised at that Bible study where my sister Stella said, 'I have a problem with the Gospel of John. The author never called himself John; rather, he always called himself, "the disciple whom Jesus loved", the "other disciple" or "the other disciple, whom Jesus loved"'. The two verses that she then quoted opened my eyes. This led me to search the scriptures, and for that I am very grateful. Your word has preserved many important details for us but I had not paid attention to them. Thankfully, she did. By raising this question she inspired me to take a closer look at the Bible on this issue and the search for truth on this question has resulted in a greater appreciation for your word.

"Teach me thy way, O LORD; I will walk in thy truth" (Ps. 86:11a).

* * * * *

Thank you to those who gave their time and resources to help in the production of this book, especially my wife Kathleen, my mother, my sisters and my friends. Your prayers, encouragement, assistance, patience and love were vital to this project and are deeply appreciated.

To those who sent funds to help print books and those who have recommended this book to others, thank you for your support. Thank you also to Meridith and Joel for our wonderful cover. My deepest appreciation also goes out to Kathleen, Clare, Lisa, Ellen, Dianne, Terry, Cherie', Barbara, John, Ron, David, Jason, Rick, Tom, and Tom, for their help, comments, and suggestions on this edition and previous editions. I also need to thank Jack, David, Mark and Luis for their contributions to this fifth edition. Truly the efforts of everyone above has worked together to produce this book. May God bless you who helped in this work, along with all who use it to honor God's word.

THE DISCIPLE WHOM JESUS LOVED

TABLE OF CONTENTS

THE TRUTH MATTERS

- Gospel of the Disciple Whom Jesus Loved
- The Integrity of the Bible
- Jury Duty
- Just the Facts and Just the Bible
- Verify – According to the Scriptures
- The Truth Is Our Goal
- Bible References and Quotes
- A Worthwhile Pursuit and a Helping Hand
- "From Heaven, or of Men?"
- The Authority of God's Word

THE DISCIPLE WHOM JESUS LOVED: WHAT DOES THE BIBLE SAY?

- "The Disciple Whom Jesus Loved"
- The "Other Disciple" of the Fourth Gospel
- A Look at the Scriptures
- A Latecomer?
- Erased from the Bible?
- A Few More Questions Before the Answers

Chapter 6 (Continued)

- Names in Scripture
- The Other Murder Plot
- Which Disciple Was Known?
- "Add Thou Not unto His Words"

THE BIBLE VERSUS TRADITION
& MORE BIBLE FACTS TO CONSIDER

- The Jury Summation
- The First Disciples
- Another Possibility
- Mark's Mystery Man
- A Fashion Statement?
- Enough Evidence?
- More than a Story?
- Who Was Jesus Speaking About?
- In Conclusion
- Where Do We Go from Here?
- Respect for the Authority of God's Word

- The "Other Disciple" Believed First
- The Bible Versus Non-Bible Sources
- A Better Bible Study Method
- "The LORD Trieth the Hearts"

PREFACE

"Every word of God *is* pure: he *is* a shield unto them that put their trust in him" (Pr. 30:5).

"Add thou not unto his words, lest he reprove thee, and thou be found a liar" (Pr. 30:6).

"There is a way that seemeth right unto a man, but the end thereof *are* the ways of death" (Pr. 16:25).

"*It is* better to trust in the LORD than to put confidence in man. *It is* better to trust in the LORD than to put confidence in princes" (Ps. 118:8-9).

"For the LORD giveth wisdom: out of his mouth *cometh* knowledge and understanding" (Pr. 2:6).

"The man that wandereth out of the way of understanding shall remain in the congregation of the dead" (Pr. 21:16).

"... Man shall not live by bread alone, but by every word that proceedeth out of the mouth of God" (Mt. 4:4b).

"As newborn babes, desire the sincere milk of the word, that ye may grow thereby..." (1Pt. 2:2a).

"For the word of the LORD *is* right..." (Ps. 33:4a).

"... he that hath my word, let him speak my word faithfully" (Jer. 23:28b).

"A faithful witness will not lie..." (Pr. 14:5a).

"Study to shew thyself approved unto God, a workman that needeth not to be ashamed..." (2Ti. 2:15a).

"Blessed is that man that maketh the LORD his trust, and respecteth not the proud, nor such as turn aside to lies" (Ps. 40:4).

"Prove all things; hold fast that which is good" (1Th. 5:21).

"*It is* the glory of God to conceal a thing: but the honour of kings *is* to search out a matter" (Pr. 25:2).

INTRODUCTION

The first three gospels all mention these three notable events of Jesus' ministry, his transfiguration (Mt. 17:1-9, Mk. 9:2-9, Lu. 9:28-36), his Gethsemane prayers (Mt. 26:36-46, Mk. 14:32-42, Lu. 22:39-46), and his raising of the daughter of Jairus (Mt. 9:18-26, Mk. 5:22-43, Lu. 8:41-56). Only three disciples were present at these events, and the Apostle John was one of them (Mt. 17:1 & 26:37, Mk. 5:37, 9:2 & 14:33, Lu. 8:51 & 9:28). Although John was an eyewitness to all of these events there is no mention of these key events in the gospel that today bears John's name! These events would surely have been extremely profound moments in John's life. So what can explain their omission from the fourth gospel, a book that tradition has said was written by John?

Many teachers will refer to the fourth gospel as 'John's eyewitness testimony', but does the Bible support this claim? A closer look shows that the idea of John being the author of the fourth gospel is not consistent with the facts found in scripture and the author's omission of the three events noted above is merely the tip of the iceberg. It turns out that **every** event where John is referred to by name in the first three gospels is missing from the fourth gospel – every one of them!

For example, Jesus told John, "ye know not what manner of spirit ye are of" when rebuking John and his brother after they sought to "command fire to come down from heaven" (Lu. 9:54-55). John and Peter were sent by Jesus to prepare the Passover (Lu. 22:8).

Jesus "privately" answered the questions of John, Peter, James, and Andrew on the Mount of Olives (Mk. 13:3). John and his brother asked Jesus to seat them, "one on thy right hand, and the other on thy left hand, in thy glory" (Mk. 10:35-41). But these events will not be found in the fourth gospel, because **none** of the events where John is named in the first three gospels are in the fourth gospel. Does its omission of all of the 'John events' support the idea that the fourth gospel is 'John's eyewitness testimony'?

If this was John's eyewitness account, how did he come to exclude all mention of these events? Are we to believe that John read the other gospels first and then wrote this gospel in such a way as to carefully omit every event where he was named in those other three gospels? Is this reasonable?

In the last chapter of the fourth gospel, verses 21:20 and 24 let us know that it was written by an unnamed "disciple whom Jesus loved". This author never identified himself as John. Rather, he used various terms like "the disciple whom Jesus loved", "the other disciple", etc. to refer to himself and his use of these curious terms to cloak his identity raises many questions.

The fourth gospel does present the author's testimony, but scripture can prove he was not John. The idea he was John came from non-Bible sources and, though there is not a single verse that justifies teaching the beloved disciple was John, this case of mistaken identity still persists. Yet whoever he was, he cannot have been John because that idea forces the Bible to contradict itself, which the truth can't do.

Lest anyone mistake the thrust of this study, note that **God's word is not in error and nothing herein suggests otherwise.** In fact, this study cites nothing but the scriptures because the Bible is the primary source on Bible issues and, if we heed the details that have been preserved therein, it can help to correct mistaken ideas that we may have. As will be shown, the title *Gospel of John* was not written by the gospel's author. Others added that title to this author's work. Still, the record of scripture is able to overcome the errors of men and the verses quoted in this study do exactly that.

Indeed, one should not be presenting an idea as if it were biblical if he cannot cite a single verse that would justify teaching that idea. Also, if the Bible can disprove an idea that we have believed, why wouldn't we give up that idea and stand corrected?

Acts 18:24-28 tells of a man named Apollos. He was "mighty in the scriptures", "instructed in the way of the Lord", "fervent in the spirit", and "spake and taught diligently the things of the Lord". Yet, we know that his understanding was lacking because when "Aquila and Priscilla had heard" his teaching, they "took him" and "expounded unto him the way of God more perfectly". [The Greek here says, "more accurately".] We are told, at that time, Apollos knew of "only the baptism of John" (i.e., John the Baptist). But the key point is that Apollos revised his teaching when the truth was presented to him. Thereafter, we are told how Apollos, "mightily convinced the Jews", "shewing by the scriptures that Jesus was Christ". Apollos was "mighty in the scriptures" and he was still willing to be taught, so, why not us?

History proves that errors can become widely accepted as truth: the 'Piltdown Man' evolution hoax, the flat earth myth, etc. Most people tend to take 'the scholars' word for it on such issues, assuming that what the 'experts' teach *is* the truth. But where Bible questions are concerned we can test if what we believe is true or not. Seeking the truth requires us to weigh the evidence without prejudice. If we are to render a fair verdict, then we must be careful not to let our judgment of the facts be distorted by ideas that we have previously assumed were true.

There is very often a difference between what people think the Bible says and what it really says. So, the way to verify the truth on biblical issues is to check to see what the Bible itself says. In this case, since the fourth gospel's author identified himself in terms of Jesus' love for him, it makes sense to see who scripture says had this relationship with Jesus. When these verses are examined one will see that **the Bible never singles out John in this manner!** Thus, unless one can show that "the disciple whom Jesus loved" was John, it is unbiblical to call John 'the beloved disciple'.

The Bible has much more for us to consider regarding this question and, thank God, the identity of the one whom "Jesus loved" can be shown from a study of the Bible facts alone. Rather than quoting non-Bible sources, the method used to shed light on the beloved disciple in this study is to just compare scripture with scripture and let God's word guide us to the truth. By doing so it is hoped that readers of this work will gain a new appreciation for the details God has preserved for us in the biblical record.

Today many people think that the Bible can't reveal anything new, because they assume that the popular teachers and scholars have already mined all of the truth out of God's word. But the evidence in this study will prove otherwise and will confirm that scripture can still provide "reproof" and "correction" (2Ti. 3:16). Let us not trust in "enticing words of man's wisdom", because our faith "should not stand in the wisdom of men, but in the power of God" (1Cor. 2:4 & 5).

What would you say to someone who asked, 'Why should people read the Bible? If the best that one can hope for is to learn what the scholars have already discovered, then why not just tell people to read the writings of the scholars, rather than reading the Bible and risk misunderstanding what it says?'

The goal of this book is to encourage a love of the truth. Lord willing, those who read this study will be led to read the Bible more, to read it more carefully, and to test the things that they are told by others, rather than just assuming them to be true. Concerning this issue, would it not be wise to heed the "prove all things" admonition (1Th. 5:21), especially since there are a number of Bible facts that do seem to argue against the John tradition?

If the evidence of scripture can disprove the John idea, then the authority of God's word provides sufficient reason for rejecting the non-Bible sources that are used to justify the John tradition. Herein, the light of scripture will expose the danger of assuming that the opinions of others can serve as a measure for determining what is true. The truth is not assured by simply following the herd.

We know many things about John: his name; that he was the son of Zebedee and had a brother named James; that he was a fisherman; that he and his brother were partners with Peter, and were there when Jesus healed Peter's wife's mother; that John was one of the twelve apostles chosen by Jesus; that John and his brother asked for the seats next to Jesus, and that Jesus surnamed them, "Boanerges, which is, The sons of thunder"; that John was there at the raising of Jairus' daughter, the transfiguration, and Jesus' prayers in the garden; that John and his brother wanted to call fire down from heaven on one group of people, and that Jesus rebuked them for it; that John was the one who told Jesus, "we saw one casting out devils in thy name; and we forbad him"; etc. (Mt. 4:21, 10:2, 17:1, 26:37, Mk. 1:19, 1:29-31, 3:17, 5:37, 9:2, 9:38, 10:35, 14:33, Lu. 5:10, 6:14, 8:51, 9:28, 9:49, 9:54-55, et al.). Yet, amazingly, **none** of this information about John can be learned from the gospel that popular opinion says was written by the Apostle John.

As will be shown in this study, the only detail that is reported in the fourth gospel that is specific to John is a notation that "the *sons* of Zebedee" were present with some fellow disciples at an event that is mentioned at the end of the book. However, since John is never named in this gospel, a person would have to know beforehand from another source that John was a son of Zebedee in order to know that the phrase "the *sons* of Zebedee" even referred to John. Therefore, it turns out that the least helpful of the four gospels when it comes to learning facts about the Apostle John and the things that he witnessed, said, and did during the ministry of Jesus, is the one that men decided to call *The Gospel of John!*

The Disciple Whom Jesus Loved

Chapter 1

THE TRUTH MATTERS

Gospel of the Disciple Whom Jesus Loved

The God-inspired writer of our fourth gospel was careful never to identify himself by name. Since he deliberately concealed his identity, then perhaps it is not wise to ignore his efforts in this regard and uncritically accept the idea that this author was the Apostle John, the brother of James, son of Zebedee. Should we not ask why God's inspired author used cryptic phrases like "the disciple whom Jesus loved" to refer to himself? Why didn't he just use his name? Paul was named repeatedly in his books and John gave his name five times in the Book of Revelation.

Instead of simply identifying himself by name this author cloaked himself in a veil of anonymity. Since God did not lead this gospel author to identify himself as John, should we be quick to follow those who tell us that he *was* the Apostle John? Non-Bible sources can be wrong. So, why wouldn't we want to see if this belief lines up with scripture – especially considering the fact that the author of this gospel went to great lengths to hide his identity?

This is not to suggest that the identity of this author cannot be determined. There is a person who does fit all that the Bible reveals about this author. Several passages in his gospel, like 20:5 and 21:21, indicate that this author was a male. Establishing his identity, however, takes a bit more effort. Therefore, this study will seek to examine everything that the Bible can tell us about this individual. We will search the scriptures for the answer to the question that the author's self-description poses to the readers of his gospel: Who was "the disciple whom Jesus loved"?

The Integrity of the Bible

The content of the fourth gospel is true and trustworthy. This is not what is in question. Nothing presented herein casts any doubt whatsoever on the legitimacy of this gospel as inspired scripture or its rightful inclusion in the New Testament. No one should think that this study in any way challenges the words of God's inspired writers or the accuracy of scripture. Any such innuendo would plainly be a flagrant distortion of what is discussed in this book.

A firm reliance on the Bible as the inspired word of God does not prohibit the questioning of the traditions of men. <u>Jesus himself was quite willing to challenge religious teachings that were based on an erroneous understanding of the scriptures</u>. It is not improper for us to question teachings or traditions, even widely accepted ones, if we discover evidence that suggests that something is amiss. If you love Jesus, then you love the truth. A search for truth, utilizing only the evidence contained in God's word, is what you will find in this study.

Jury Duty

As you read on act as if you are on a jury and that the Bible is Exhibit A. Your job is to weigh the testimony of scripture and decide whether or not this evidence is able to meet the burden of proof in two cases, both involving the identity of "the disciple whom Jesus loved". You are the one who will render the verdict in these matters, so it is up to you to prayerfully seek the truth and consider the evidence without prejudice.

In the first case this study will seek to prove beyond a reasonable doubt that the Apostle John was not "the disciple whom Jesus loved". Although beyond a reasonable doubt is a very high standard the biblical evidence presented in this case should be sufficient to meet this standard, in your judgment. The facts will prove that the Apostle John and this unnamed author were two different individuals.

The second case seeks to prove the identity of this heretofore misidentified disciple, but only to a preponderance of the evidence. (This simply means the greater weight of evidence, enough to 'tip the scales' or to prove that something is more likely true than not true.) But, here too, it is up to you to decide if the evidence offered on this point is sufficient.

Just the Facts and Just the Bible

As was stated earlier, the writer of this gospel always described himself with phrases that avoided directly disclosing his identity. When one takes note of this, then mere dogmatic assertions regarding this author's identity will probably sound less convincing than they would have otherwise sounded, given that his identity was the very thing that God saw fit to have him conceal. However, as you will soon see, the scriptures can reveal as well as conceal.

Those new to the Bible may be unaware that this gospel's inspired author did not entitle his work *The Gospel of John*. That title (like the chapter and verse divisions) was not in the author's original text. It was added to his book by others and it is evident that title was not a product of the inspired author, for the author surely did not proclaim his name in a title since the cumbersome terms that the author used to refer to himself in the gospel plainly indicate that he intended to conceal his identity.

All scripture is inspired by God, but hearsay tradition is not. So, this study will not cite non-Bible sources like the opinions of scholars or comments attributed to this-or-that person in the 'early' church or the writings of men from the present or the past. Man's wisdom is not God's wisdom, so <u>non-Bible sources ought to be viewed in light of scripture and **not** the other way around</u>. Therefore, only scripture and the logical results of comparing scripture with scripture will be offered as evidence in this book.

<u>Verify – According to the Scriptures</u>

In Acts 17:11 we are told the Bereans, "were more noble than those in Thessalonica, in that they received the word with all readiness of mind, and searched the scriptures daily, whether those things were so" and we, too, can be diligent in seeking the truth by testing every idea against the word of God.

If we read a book or hear a teaching, then we can subject those ideas to biblical scrutiny (in line with the directive "prove all things" (1Th. 5:21)). It was Paul who taught the Bereans and even though he was an apostle they still "searched the scriptures" – and they were praised for doing so! Therefore, it is fair to hold our teachers to the same standard. We can be just as conscientious in our pursuit of truth because we can use the Bible to test our beliefs and the ideas that are presented to us.

Christians have nothing to fear from the truth. But since new ideas challenge tradition, they are often mocked or simply dismissed. However, unless man has discovered all of the truth in the Bible, then we should always be open to the possibility that God may, at times, have something new to teach us.

The Truth Is Our Goal

God surely knew that inspiring this author to refer to himself as "the disciple whom Jesus loved" would cause some to wonder about his identity. So, let's look to the Bible to see if we can ascertain who this anonymous author was. In seeking to answer this question do not just assume that you can trust the opinion of others more than your own. Popular opinion can be wrong. Even if 'everybody' thinks something is true that does not make it so. If 'all' the scholars said the earth is flat and they ridiculed anyone who dared to question their 'accepted *truth*', they would nevertheless be wrong.

Let's follow the example of the Bereans. They didn't just take Paul's word for it. They searched the scriptures – and we should do likewise when we are taught '"the disciple whom Jesus loved" was John'. The incredible thing is that there's not a single verse that would justify teaching that idea! In spite of this, commentaries and teachers will habitually say that 'John was the beloved disciple' and they state this **as if it were biblical**. In reality, however, all such assertions amount to opinion being mistakenly sold as fact. In this Bible study you will see for yourself what happens when the John tradition is put to the test of scripture.

Commentaries or other books can be helpful, especially when they highlight some details we might otherwise miss. But we need to test the statements they make and you should treat this book likewise. Carefully evaluate the two cases that are presented in this study and verify each scripture reference.

While the verses needed for this study are quoted herein, looking them up will enable you to confirm the evidence in its context. By doing so, you will become more grounded in God's word, even as you are built up in both confidence and competence when it comes to discussing the topic of this study.

Also, Proverbs 3:5-6 says, "Trust in the LORD with all thine heart; and lean not unto thine own understanding. In all thy ways acknowledge him, and he shall direct thy paths". So, rather than cling to our understanding of things, we should trust in the LORD and follow wherever the truth in his word takes us.

Bible References and Quotes

This study will quote only the Holy Bible as previously noted. Yet, the wording in your Bible may vary on some of these quotes, since there are many different versions of the Bible. Still, no matter which Bible version you use you will be able to verify the accuracy and context of every passage cited. The differences in wording between Bible versions won't alter the verdict that is demanded by the evidence.

All of the quotes in this study are taken from the King James Version (KJV). While the KJV can be challenging at times it remains the most widely held

Bible version, so it will be the one quoted. Thus, you will find some words that appear to be misspelled, like "shewed". These are not errors but are the result of exactly quoting the KJV. (Herein the marks "" will be reserved solely for direct quotations of scripture. Also, for clarification, ten Greek terms are included from the *Interlinear Greek-English New Testament*, published by Baker Book House, 1981.)

A Worthwhile Pursuit and a Helping Hand

Rather than dive into God's word to see if the John idea is true or not some try to dodge the issue by asking: 'What difference does it make?' Well, for starters, if the John idea isn't true, then promoting it undercuts the authority of scripture (just like every false idea that men ascribe to God's word). In fact it will be shown that the John tradition actually makes scripture contradict itself, which the truth cannot do. A more in-depth answer to this question follows later, but for now let it suffice that Jesus clearly indicated the truth matters (Fourth gospel 8:32, 14:6, 17:17, 18:37, et al.).

Proverbs 2:3-5 establishes that the pursuit of knowledge is a worthwhile endeavor and the source that we should look to is suggested in the next verse – "For the LORD giveth wisdom: out of his mouth *cometh* knowledge and understanding" (Pr. 2:6). Still, this pursuit is not a task that one needs to take on alone. The Holy Spirit was called "the Spirit of truth" when Jesus told the disciples, "he will guide you into all truth" (Fourth gospel 16:13) and Jesus said the Father would, "give the Holy Spirit to them that ask him" (Lu. 11:13). So, we should ask the Father for help if we want the Spirit to guide our study of scripture.

"From Heaven, or of Men?"

Truth is not a minor issue. When Jesus said, "no man cometh unto the Father, but by me", he did so in the context of identifying himself as, "the truth" (Fourth gospel 14:6). He also said, "God *is* a Spirit: and they that worship him must worship *him* in spirit and in truth" (Fourth gospel 4:24). So, clearly, "truth" is not an optional item or a 'secondary' matter. Furthermore, scripture encourages speaking the truth (Pr. 12:17 & 19, Zec. 8:16, Eph. 4:15 & 25), ties sanctification and growth to truth (Fourth gospel 17:17 & 19, Eph. 4:15, 2Th. 2:13, Jam. 1:18, 1Pt. 1:22), links the armor of God and fruit of the spirit to truth (Eph. 5:9 & 6:14), and Psalm 145:18 says, "the LORD *is* nigh unto all them that call upon him, to all that call upon him in truth". If a relationship with God is to be fruitful, respect for truth seems to be vital.

Those who seek the truth would do well to note the test of authority that we see used by Jesus. When the religious leaders questioned the authority of Jesus, he pointed to one's **source** as a litmus test on authority when he responded with this question about John the Baptist, "The baptism of John, was it from heaven, or of men?" (Lu. 20:4). Of course, if it was "from heaven", then his source was God. So, in order to avoid facing the truth they had to dodge the issue, since they had refused to believe John (cf. Lu. 20:5-7), and he testified of Jesus. In our case, this test helps one to properly weigh the evidence by considering its source: Was it from heaven, or of men? Keep this in mind as you weigh the words of scripture herein. Many don't take time to consider the source, but this simple test can help to keep us focused on the fact God's word is true and it is worthy of our respect.

We will revisit this test later and at that time we will consider how the truth is often used by God to prove what is in the heart of man. Those who love God will accept the authority of God's word on issues where its truth challenges their belief.

The Authority of God's Word

Jesus said, "He that is of God heareth God's words" (Fourth gospel 8:47). So, the words of scripture should be enough to move us to stand with the truth. When the word of God offers to correct us, we ought to be humble enough to admit that we were wrong, but clearly not all will do so. Proverbs 1:29-30 tells of those who, "hated knowledge, and did not choose the fear of the LORD: They would none of my counsel: they despised all my reproof" and some people still respond in this way to God's word today. Sadly, the reaction to truth in our day is far too often precisely like the response the LORD described in Jeremiah 19:15, "they have hardened their necks, that they might not hear my words."

"*It is* better to trust in the LORD than to put confidence in man" (Ps. 118:8). So, unlike those who try to defend the John idea by urging people to rely on non-Bible sources, this work will quote the Bible only. That way the authority of God's word can provide the boldness needed to stand corrected and witness to the truth, even in the face of ridicule from those who are wedded to tradition and don't want to admit that their trust in non-Bible sources was misplaced.

"The fear of man bringeth a snare: but whoso putteth his trust in the LORD shall be safe" (Pr. 29:25).

Chapter 2

THE DISCIPLE WHOM JESUS LOVED: WHAT DOES THE BIBLE SAY?

"The Disciple Whom Jesus Loved"

The fourth gospel was written by "the disciple whom Jesus loved" (Fourth gospel 21:20 & 24). This was how the author referred to himself, along with the "other disciple", "the other disciple, whom Jesus loved", etc. and his use of these anonymous terms should prompt us to ask questions, such as: Other than who? (Note: this author is never identified as an "apostle".) Merely declaring this was John does not make it true and it is a logical fallacy to assume that the majority's opinion must be right. So, we should let scripture be the standard by which truth is judged when it comes to the identity of this gospel author.

The phrase "the disciple whom Jesus loved" is notable for several reasons but primarily because it means that his relationship with Jesus was unique. He is set apart from the rest of the disciples of Jesus as "the disciple" (singular) that has the distinction of being identified as the one whom "Jesus loved".

If you met a man who referred to himself as 'the one my mother loved' you would surely wonder why he did so. This phrase suggests a distinctive relationship and, if it is true, it would indicate that his mother had a unique connection with him. So, when the Bible calls someone "the disciple whom Jesus loved" it should arrest our attention. As the author of the fourth gospel used this term to refer to himself it is fair to ask: What could have led him to do so? Since this curious phrase distinguishes the author based on the unique regard that Jesus had for him, should we not wonder why God's word took the time to highlight Jesus' relationship with this author?

The designation "the disciple whom Jesus loved" differentiates this disciple on the basis of Jesus' relationship to him. This is not the same as his love *for* Jesus and the use of that term means Jesus' love for this disciple is a distinguishing factor or else the phrase is stripped of its meaning.

Since the Bible emphasizes this relationship with Jesus, it is logical to search the scriptures for evidence of such a relationship in Jesus' life. This is precisely what we will do. Let us begin by probing every passage that mentions this unnamed disciple so we can get to know him a little better.

The "Other Disciple" of the Fourth Gospel

The author first differentiated himself from the rest of the disciples when he wrote, "Now there was leaning on Jesus' bosom one of his disciples, whom Jesus loved" (Fourth gospel 13:23). Then, when Jesus was being put on trial, this author said that Peter and "another disciple" showed up, who is also called "that other disciple" (Fourth gospel 18:15 & 16). [The literal Greek here reads, "the other disciple" in 18:15 and, "the disciple other" in 18:16.] Following this, when Jesus was on the cross, the author wrote that Jesus "saw his mother and the disciple standing by, whom he loved". This is the one who the author also called, "the disciple" and "that disciple" (Fourth gospel 19:26 & 27). The author then wove together his terms and used "the other disciple, whom Jesus loved", along with "that other disciple", "the other disciple", and "that other disciple which came first to the sepulchre" in recounting his experiences on resurrection morning (Fourth gospel 20:2, 3, 4 & 8).

This disciple was last mentioned when the author wrote about seven disciples who went fishing together. Jesus visited them and the author says he ("that disciple whom Jesus loved") was the first to recognize Jesus (Fourth gospel 21:7). A few verses later he was also called "the disciple whom Jesus loved" and it was confirmed that he was the one "which also leaned on his breast at supper and said, Lord, which is he that betrayeth thee?" (Fourth gospel 21:20). The terms "him", "this man", "he", and "that disciple" were next used to refer to him (Fourth gospel 21:21-23). The author then wrote, "This is the disciple which testifieth of these things, and wrote these things" (Fourth gospel 21:24). The context reveals he is the one called "that disciple" in verse 23 and "the disciple whom Jesus loved" in verse 20.

The preceding references make it clear that "whom Jesus loved" was the most revealing term that this author used to refer to himself. If the Bible calls someone "the disciple whom Jesus loved" it is reasonable to expect that he was involved in more than just Jesus' last days on this earth. Given the uniqueness of this designation he undoubtedly had a significant role in the life of Jesus. Moreover, he absolutely must have interacted with Jesus prior to the Last Supper.

Admittedly, these references let us know the author was present for some notable moments of Jesus' ministry: his last Passover, his crucifixion, and his vacant tomb on resurrection morning. But now carefully read each of the following passages and then consider them together. **What is missing?**

A Look at the Scriptures

Fourth gospel 13:21-28 (with Jesus at the supper)
Fourth gospel 18:12-18 (with Jesus at his trial)
Fourth gospel 19:25-27 (with Jesus at the cross)
Fourth gospel 20:1-10   (first man at Jesus' tomb &
                                    first to believe)
Fourth gospel 21:2-24   (first to identify Jesus &
                                    author of this gospel)

For your convenience, each of these passages is reprinted here with bold typeface highlighting all of the references to "the disciple whom Jesus loved".

13:21-28: "When Jesus had thus said, he was troubled in spirit, and testified, and said, Verily, verily, I say unto you, that one of you shall betray me. Then the disciples looked one on another, doubting of whom he spake. Now there was leaning on Jesus' bosom **one of his disciples, whom Jesus loved**. Simon Peter therefore beckoned to **him**, that **he** should ask who it should be of whom he spake. **He then lying on Jesus' breast** saith unto him, Lord, who is it? Jesus answered, He it is, to whom I shall give a sop, when I have dipped *it*. And when he had dipped the sop, he gave *it* to Judas Iscariot, *the son* of Simon. And after the sop Satan entered into him. Then said Jesus unto him, That thou doest, do quickly. Now no man at the table knew for what intent he spake this unto him."

18:12-18: "Then the band and the captain and officers of the Jews took Jesus, and bound him, And led him away to Annas first; for he was father in law to Caiaphas, which was the high priest that same year. Now Caiaphas was he, which gave counsel to the Jews, that it was expedient that one man should die for the people. And Simon Peter followed Jesus, and *so did* **another disciple**: **that disciple** was known unto the high priest, and went in with Jesus into the palace of the high priest. But Peter stood at the door without. Then went out **that other disciple**, which was known unto the high priest, and spake unto her that kept the door, and brought in Peter. Then saith the damsel that kept the door unto Peter, Art not thou also *one* of this man's disciples? He saith, I am not. And the servants and officers stood there, who had made a fire of coals; for it was cold: and they warmed themselves: and Peter stood with them, and warmed himself."

19:25-27: "Now there stood by the cross of Jesus his mother, and his mother's sister, Mary the *wife* of Cleophas, and Mary Magdalene. When Jesus therefore saw his mother, and **the disciple standing by, whom he loved**, he saith unto his mother, Woman, behold thy son! Then saith he to **the disciple**, Behold thy mother! And from that hour **that disciple** took her unto **his** own *home*."

20:1-10: "The first *day* of the week cometh Mary Magdalene early, when it was yet dark, unto the sepulchre, and seeth the stone taken away from the sepulchre. Then she runneth, and cometh to Simon Peter, and to **the other disciple, whom Jesus loved**, and saith unto them, They have taken away the Lord out of the sepulchre, and we know not where they have laid him. Peter therefore went forth, and **that other disciple**, and came to the sepulchre. So they ran both together: and **the other disciple** did outrun Peter, and came first to the sepulchre. And **he** stooping down, *and looking in*, saw the linen clothes lying; yet went **he** not in. Then cometh Simon Peter following **him**, and went into the sepulchre, and seeth the linen clothes lie, And the napkin, that was about his head, not lying with the linen clothes, but wrapped together in a place by itself. Then went in also **that other disciple, which came first to the sepulchre**, and **he** saw, and believed. For as yet they knew not the scripture, that he must rise again from the dead. Then the disciples went away again unto their own home."

21:2-24: "There were together Simon Peter, and Thomas called Didymus, and Nathanael of Cana in Galilee, and the *sons* of Zebedee, and two other of his disciples. Simon Peter saith unto them, I go a fishing. They say unto him, We also go with thee. They went forth, and entered into a ship immediately; and that night they caught nothing. But when the morning was now come, Jesus stood on the shore: but the disciples knew not that it was Jesus. Then Jesus saith unto them, Children, have ye any meat? They answered him, No. And he said unto them, Cast the net on the right side of the ship, and ye shall find. They cast therefore, and now they were not able to draw it for the multitude of fishes. Therefore **that disciple whom Jesus loved** saith unto Peter, It is the Lord. Now when Simon Peter heard that it was the Lord, he girt *his* fisher's coat *unto him*, (for he was naked,) and did cast himself into the sea. And the other disciples came in a little ship; (for they were not far from land, but as it were two hundred cubits,) dragging the net with fishes. As soon then as they were come to land, they saw a fire of coals there, and fish laid thereon, and bread. Jesus saith unto them, Bring of the fish which ye have now caught. Simon Peter went up, and drew the net to land full of great fishes, an hundred and fifty and three: and for all there were so many, yet was not the net broken. Jesus saith unto them, Come *and* dine. And none of the disciples durst ask him, Who art thou? knowing that it was the Lord. Jesus then cometh, and taketh bread, and giveth them, and fish likewise. This is now the third time that Jesus shewed himself to his disciples, after that he was risen from the dead. So when they had dined, Jesus saith to Simon Peter, Simon, *son* of Jonas, lovest thou me more than these? He saith unto him, Yea, Lord; thou knowest that I love thee. He saith unto him, Feed my lambs. He saith to him again the second time, Simon, *son* of Jonas, lovest thou me? He saith unto him, Yea, Lord; thou knowest that I love thee. He saith unto him, Feed my sheep. He saith unto him the third time, Simon, *son* of Jonas, lovest thou me? Peter was grieved because he said unto him the third time, Lovest thou me? And he said unto him, Lord, thou knowest all things; thou knowest that I love thee. Jesus saith unto him, Feed my sheep. Verily, verily, I say unto thee, When thou wast young, thou girdedst thyself, and walkedst whither thou wouldest: but when thou shalt be old, thou shalt stretch forth thy hands, and another shall gird thee, and carry *thee* whither thou wouldest not. This spake he, signifying by what death he should glorify God. And when he had spoken this, he saith unto him, Follow me. Then Peter, turning about, seeth **the disciple whom Jesus loved** following; which also leaned on his breast at supper, and said, Lord, which is he that betrayeth thee? Peter seeing **him** saith to Jesus, Lord, and what *shall* **this man** *do*? Jesus saith unto him, If I will that **he** tarry till I come, what *is that* to thee? follow thou me. Then went this saying abroad among the brethren, that **that disciple** should not die: yet Jesus said not unto him, **He** shall not die; but, If I will that **he** tarry till I come, what *is that* to thee? **This is the disciple which testifieth of these things**, and wrote these things: and we know that **his** testimony is true."

A Latecomer?

The most unusual thing about the author is that he seems to appear unexpectedly from out of nowhere. It should arrest our attention when we first find out that there is no mention of anyone called "the disciple whom Jesus loved" prior to chapter 13 of the fourth gospel. This person's history with Jesus is missing! Why?

The very first time that we read about this one unnamed disciple whom "Jesus loved" is at Jesus' last Passover. (At that event the rest of the disciples worried that they might be the betrayer and Peter eventually urged the one whom "Jesus loved" to ask Jesus who the betrayer would be.) Before this episode we do not find the terms "other disciple" or "the disciple whom Jesus loved" in the fourth gospel. What can account for this?

It does not make sense that someone could suddenly appear on the scene during the last days of Jesus' earthly ministry and just instantly become "the disciple whom Jesus loved".

The "other disciple" had a special relationship with Jesus and that degree of friendship does not materialize out of thin air. So why do the scriptural references to this unnamed disciple seem to begin on the day before Jesus is killed? The questions get even more curious.

The terms "the disciple whom Jesus loved", "other disciple", etc. appear in only five passages of scripture (those being the ones just quoted above). Why? Surely someone who was close enough to Jesus to be called "the disciple whom Jesus loved" had to have been interacting with Jesus before that last Passover. Yet, we find no prior mention of an unnamed "disciple whom Jesus loved" in the book that he himself wrote. So where should we look?

Erased from the Bible?

The bad news is that no other books of the Bible contain any reference to any person called "the disciple whom Jesus loved". You will not find this phrase outside of this author's own gospel. As a matter of fact, the other three gospel writers avoided mentioning the presence of this "other disciple" even when we know for certain that he was present!

For example, all four gospels note that Peter followed Jesus into the palace of the high priest on the night of Jesus' arrest. But the first three gospels totally ignore the "other disciple", who <u>was</u> there and who got Peter through the door. Since no one else is mentioned in those reports, someone reading one or all of those accounts might think it safe to assume that Peter was alone when this occurred. Wrong!

We know that Peter and the "other disciple" **both** followed Jesus that night (Fourth gospel 18:15-16). But there is no mention of this "other disciple" in either Matthew 26:58, Mark 14:54, or Luke 22:54-55, all of which tell only of Peter's following Jesus on that night. Why would the writers of those gospels purposely omit the presence of the "other disciple"?

Why would "the disciple whom Jesus loved" get no visible mention outside of his own gospel? He was very close to Jesus and played a role during several of the weightiest moments of Jesus' life. He was the author of one of the four gospels. Yet, **if we didn't have his gospel, we would not know about Jesus' unique relationship with him nor would we have any way to know that he even existed!** Doesn't this seem strange to you?

The fact the other three gospels never refer to the one whom "Jesus loved", "other disciple", etc. is significant. You'll soon see that this "otherdisciple" was set apart from the rest of the disciples in a very special way by the actions of Jesus – a key piece of evidence that will help us to identify him.

A Few More Questions Before the Answers

This unnamed disciple did not just suddenly pop up in the days before Jesus was killed. So then why does it appear this way in scripture? Why did "the disciple whom Jesus loved" write his gospel in such a way that he seems to come from out of nowhere? The scriptures suggest a reason, one that will also help to prove the author's identity.

What can we learn from the fact that the first mention of this unnamed disciple doesn't occur until chapter 13 of the fourth gospel? Why did the author of the fourth gospel choose that point in his own gospel narrative to start referring to himself?

Chapter 13 tells us a lot about Jesus' last Passover but it does not explain either the timing of, or the reason for, the sudden appearance of the one whom "Jesus loved". Still, there is a significant event recorded in the Bible that does help to answer each of the foregoing questions and that event occurred just prior to that same Passover. We will focus on that episode a little bit later. First, though, let's take a closer look at the Apostle John.

Chapter 3

THE EVIDENCE PRO & CON: WAS JOHN THE BELOVED DISCIPLE?

The Testimony of Scripture Regarding John

There is no evidence John ever claimed to be the author of the fourth gospel, so the fact it came to bear his name was not his fault. That was caused by others erroneously attributing it to him.

Certainly the Apostle John cannot be blamed for the mistakes of others and he obviously is not available to testify on this issue. But God's word has preserved a body of clear and convincing evidence that is able to set the record straight in this instance.

Let us begin by looking to see what the Bible reveals about John, the brother of James and son of Zebedee. We will contrast those facts with the facts in scripture about "the disciple whom Jesus loved". As we do time and again you will see the evidence indicates that John and "the disciple whom Jesus loved" were two different people.

We will be analyzing a lot of data about "the disciple whom Jesus loved" as we go through this process. You will also be learning many of the facts that are needed to establish the true identity of this "other disciple" as we take the time to learn exactly how the evidence 'clears' John.

How Humble Was the Apostle John?

The belief that John was the author of the fourth gospel is typically defended with this excuse: 'John didn't identify himself as the author because he wanted to be humble.' Is this reasonable?

John named himself five times in the Book of Revelation. Does this mean he was more prideful (or less humble)? Surely not. But this contrast does argue against the idea the same man also wrote the fourth gospel – John's identity was <u>repeatedly noted</u> in the Book of Revelation, while in the fourth gospel the identity of the author was <u>repeatedly obscured</u>. Moreover, "the disciple whom Jesus loved" is not the most humble-sounding self-description. If it were not part of scripture the author's use of this designation might actually seem to be quite immodest. Rather than refer to himself by repeatedly mentioning that Jesus loved him, if this writer had just used his name would it really seem less humble? (Those who try to attribute this gospel to John offer no logical reason why John would have sought to conceal his identity. But it turns out that something recorded in scripture about the actual author gives us at least one reason why he might avoid identifying himself by name.)

The notion that 'humility was the reason that John did not use his name' has other shortcomings. Consider what the Bible tells us about John and his brother. Jesus named them, "The sons of thunder" (Mk. 3:17). We are told that they sought power to call fire down from heaven to consume people (Lu. 9:54). They also proposed that **they** should be the ones sitting on the right hand and left hand of Jesus in his kingdom (Mk. 10:35-40). Does that sound like humility? Their fellow apostles did not seem to think so for it goes on to say, "when the ten heard *it* they began to be much displeased with James and John" (Mk. 10:41). Clearly, it was not humbleness on the part of John and his brother that caused this indignation among the rest of "the twelve"! Rather, it was a lack thereof.

Of course, this does not mean that John was never humble. But the foregoing facts were brought up merely to show that the Bible does not give us any reason to believe John was unusually humble. Prior to the day of Pentecost at least, it seems that humility was not John's strong point. Although the presence of the Holy Spirit after Pentecost naturally would have led the apostles to be more humble that does not permit us to assume unfounded actions on the part of John or any other apostle or disciple.

John was named five times in the Book of Revelation and some of the other writers of scripture named themselves in their books but that does not mean they were not humble. In addition, nothing in scripture indicates the Apostle John had reason to, or ever tried to, conceal his identity. So, the notion that 'the author of the fourth gospel is referred to as "the disciple whom Jesus loved" just because John wanted to be humble' turns out to have absolutely **no** scriptural support whatsoever.

A Glaring Oversight?

A simple truth can sometimes go unnoticed but when we realize it or when it is pointed out to us then we wonder how we could have ever missed it. Consider, for example, the other books of the Bible that are traditionally attributed to the Apostle John. Guess what is missing from all of them? None of those books ever call the Apostle John "the disciple whom Jesus loved"! Neither does any other book in the Bible. But if, as the tradition of men claims, the Apostle John wrote the gospel that bears his name, then what can explain this glaring contrast?

Those who claim that the Apostle John wrote the fourth gospel lack a plausible explanation as to why the identifying term "Jesus loved" and this key relationship were never associated with John by any writer of scripture. Moreover, those who believe that both the fourth gospel and the Book of Revelation were written by the Apostle John cannot explain why he named himself in one book and not the other. Then again, it might just be that John was not called the one whom "Jesus loved" anywhere in scripture simply because John was **not** "the disciple whom Jesus loved". So perhaps this "other disciple" was someone else, someone other than "the twelve".

Why Include John but Exclude the One Whom "Jesus Loved"?

The other gospels treat John and "the disciple whom Jesus loved" very differently. John and his brother upset the rest of the apostles on at least one occasion (Mk. 10:41). Yet the other gospel writers had no problem including John. Excluding references to John the Baptist, John was named a total of twenty times in their gospels. (He was referred to only once in the fourth gospel and we will consider this later.)

The other gospels talk of Jesus taking aside "Peter and James and John" (Mt. 17:1, Mk. 14:33, Lu. 8:51, et al.) and each one mentions other things about John. Time and again the first three gospels note John's presence and/or his actions at various events. So, the writers of those gospels were more than willing to talk about John's involvement in Jesus' ministry. But there is something incredibly peculiar about this. Do you see the problem this presents?

The other three gospel writers never refer to the one whom "Jesus loved", the "other disciple", etc. As was noted earlier, they do not mention him **even when we know that he was present** (i.e., Fourth gospel 18:15-16 as contrasted with Mt. 26:58, Mk. 14:54, & Lu. 22:54-55). So, while the other gospel writers do mention John, "the disciple whom Jesus loved" is conspicuous by his absence from their books. If he was John, then this inconsistent treatment presents a problem. Did the other three gospel writers freely mention John, except for all those times when the fourth gospel happens to mention "the disciple whom Jesus loved", the "other disciple", etc? How could they have known when to leave him out? Even if they all had a copy of the fourth gospel to know when it referred to this unnamed disciple it does not follow that they would omit all mention of him if he was John. However, if they knew he and John were two different people, then this dissimilar treatment is understandable.

Also, Matthew 27:56 tells us, "the mother of Zebedee's children" was present when Jesus died (but never mentions her son John). Yet "the disciple whom Jesus loved" **was** at the cross. So, those who say he was John are inevitably forced to believe that this author felt the presence of John's mother was worthy of mention *but her son the Apostle should be left out of the same account.* Is that reasonable? In Matthew 20:20, "the mother of Zebedee's children" was also mentioned. But there the author included "her sons" (John and James) and their conversation with Jesus (Mt. 20:20-24). So, since John was included with his mother when this author named her earlier, would he have named her while ignoring John (in his account of Jesus' death) if John had been there?

Does the work of the other gospel writers support a conclusion that the "other disciple, whom Jesus loved" and John were the same person? No, it does not, and those who claim that John was the "other disciple" cannot explain this discrepancy.

The other three gospels omit the one whom "Jesus loved", but we find many references to John in those gospels. This distinct treatment suggests that these were different people, not the same individual. Conversely, if they were two different people, then it makes sense that we would find the gospel writers treating them differently.

The Relationship Between Jesus and John

It has been taught by some that Jesus had an 'inner circle' of disciples because the Bible records three times when only "Peter and James and John" were permitted to accompany Jesus (Mt. 17:1, Mk. 13:3 & 14:33, Lu. 8:51). These three occasions were mentioned briefly in the last section. No doubt, being selected to be with Jesus at these moments was a privilege that Peter, James, and John enjoyed over the rest of the disciples.

We need to consider John's inclusion in this so-called 'inner circle' because this idea has been used by some as a rationale for supposing that John must be "the disciple whom Jesus loved". They say this means John had a special relationship with Jesus, which then leads them to assume the phrase "the disciple whom Jesus loved" is talking about the Apostle John. This, unfortunately, is not good logic nor is it scriptural.

First, John wasn't alone with Jesus on those three occasions. Thus, if being included in those events does imply an 'inner circle' relationship, then that is also true for Peter and James. In any case, nothing suggests that John's relationship with Jesus put him in a class above Peter and James or that John's relationship with Jesus was otherwise unique among the apostles.

Jesus did choose Peter and John to prepare his last Passover (Lu. 22:8). However, this one verse is not enough to justify teaching that Peter and John were the two closest disciples of Jesus. Regardless, many do believe the two closest disciples of Jesus were Peter and John, but this is because they have already been taught John *was* "the disciple whom Jesus loved". This idea is so pervasive most do not notice when circular reasoning is used to argue for John being "the disciple whom Jesus loved" – e.g., 'Peter and John were the closest ones to Jesus and Peter wasn't "the other disciple", so it must be John.' While, it is true Peter was not "the disciple whom Jesus loved" (Fourth gospel 13:23-24, 20:3 & 21:20), this line of reasoning still tells us nothing about John because the whole argument rests on a false premise.

While superficial arguments can help to sell the idea that John was the one whom "Jesus loved", the evidence suggests otherwise. In fact, there is no biblical reason to assume this anonymous disciple was an apostle or that he was one of the three men that joined Jesus on the three occasions that were discussed above. As you will see, the author called himself the "other disciple" for a very good reason – because he was "other" than "the twelve".

Peter Was Foremost Among the Twelve

Peter was the first disciple who was focused on, Jesus told Peter to feed his sheep, Jesus called Peter blessed, an angel mentioned Peter by name on resurrection morning, and it was Peter who gave an answer to the mockers on the Day of Pentecost (Fourth gospel 1:42 & 21:15-17, Mt. 16:1, Mk. 16:7, Acts 2:14). It is apparent from these and other passages that Peter was the apostle who stood out among "the twelve".

One would expect Peter to stand out from the rest of "the twelve" because that fits with what the scriptures reveal about him. Yet, this cannot be said when it comes to John. When Jesus was arrested, his disciples fled (Mt. 26:56, Mk. 14:50). After that, Peter at least somehow found the courage to follow Jesus (Fourth gospel 18:15, Mt. 26:58, Mk. 14:54, Lu. 22:54), although his three denials did begin soon thereafter.

Among "the twelve" apostles it was not John but Peter who had a notable relationship with Jesus (but, as noted earlier, Peter was not "the disciple whom Jesus loved"). Before Pentecost John was not singled out in this way in scripture, and while Jesus did take aside Peter, James, and John three times, John's actions in the four gospels do not suggest that he was a cut above the rest of "the twelve".

Conversely, the scriptures do imply that "the disciple whom Jesus loved" **was** a cut above the rest of the disciples, and we will go into detail about this later. Furthermore, a unique and very close relationship with Jesus is precisely what the term "the disciple whom Jesus loved" is acknowledging.

Do the three times when Jesus took aside Peter, James and John provide a basis to claim John was the one whom "Jesus loved"? It would be a huge stretch to make such an assumption but without it the case *for* John goes nowhere.

The Behavior and Character of John

Now we will compare the character of John to what we are told about the "other disciple, whom Jesus loved" (and remember we are talking about the pre-Pentecost Apostle John). First, let's consider the behavior of John during one of the key events in Jesus' life. The Bible reveals that when Jesus went to the Garden of Gethsemane, he specifically asked for John's support. Matthew 26:37 says Jesus, "took with him Peter and the two sons of Zebedee and began to be sorrowful and very heavy". Then Jesus had a simple request, "watch" (Mt. 26:38, Mk.14:34).

Sadly Peter, James and John could not even stay awake for Jesus while he spent time in prayer. When Jesus returned and found them sleeping, he made his dismay clear when he said to Peter, "could ye not watch with me one hour?" (Mt. 26:40, Mk. 14:37). Jesus left to pray again, and John let him down a second time. When Jesus came back that time, he "found them asleep again" (Mt. 26:43, Mk.14:40). The last time he stepped away to pray, they fell asleep also (Mt. 26:45, Mk.14:41). John acted like his fellow apostles when things were calm and the three of them failed to stay awake and watch. So, why would he have acted differently from them after the trouble started? The ensuing trial and crucifixion of Jesus were very traumatic events and, during that period, the rest of the apostles (excluding Judas) would not have been exempt from being gripped by the same fear that ultimately drove Peter to deny he even knew Jesus (Mt. 26:69-74).

Matthew 26:37-45 and Mark 14:33-41 give us a sense of just how much Peter, James, and John disappointed Jesus in the Garden of Gethsemane that night. Jesus knew Judas had betrayed him and he knew he would soon be killed. But Jesus' urgent requests were not able to rouse Peter, James, and John to action. Immediately following that series of failures by the three so-called 'inner circle' apostles, an armed and hostile mob showed up, seized Jesus, and hauled him off to trial.

If John could not manage to "watch" as Jesus had requested at Gethsemane, why would we think that John abruptly changed and began to act *unlike* his fellow apostles after Jesus was seized? There is no reason to believe John acted any differently than the way the rest of the apostles acted on that night. But the "other disciple" **did** act differently that night. We are told he, "went in with Jesus into the palace of the high priest" (Fourth gospel 18:15) and at the cross the following morning, scripture tells us that Jesus saw "the disciple standing by, whom he loved" (Fourth gospel 19:26). So, this disciple most likely stayed in the vicinity of Jesus in the period of time that transpired in between these two verses.

What would an unbiased jury conclude if they compared the behavior of the "other disciple" to that of the Apostle John – who had been unable to even stay awake for Jesus earlier on that same night?

The Bible Presents a Contrast

The Apostle John let Jesus down three times on the night that Jesus was arrested. But, later that same night, the "other disciple" showed up and went in with Jesus and, the following morning, the disciple "whom he loved" was standing at the cross of Jesus. This is a stark contrast. Given the foregoing facts ask yourself, Does the evidence really suggest John and the "other disciple" were the same person, or is it indicating they were more likely two different men? If we set aside the John idea (that non-Bible sources lead everyone to take for granted) and just compare scripture with scripture, what answer do we find the Bible pointing to?

The loyalty exhibited by the "other disciple" sets him apart from his fellow disciples. Moreover, Jesus entrusted his mother to this unnamed disciple at the cross (Fourth gospel 19:26-27a) and it says, "from that hour that disciple took her unto his own *home*" (Fourth gospel 19:27b). ("Unto his own" translates a term that the author also used in 16:32, where he clearly tied it to a change in location. So, 19:27 indicates they departed from the vicinity of the cross at that point.) Then on resurrection morning this disciple was the first man at Jesus' tomb. Furthermore, when he entered into the tomb scripture tells us he, "believed" – the first disciple after the resurrection to do so (Fourth gospel 20:2-4 & 8). Although all of this does speak well of the "other disciple", it does not in any way suggest this person was John. On the contrary, the facts in evidence indicate the "other disciple" and John were two different individuals, because they behaved differently!

"And They All Forsook Him and Fled"

It is true the "other disciple" was not the only one to show some courage after the disciples fled on the night Jesus was arrested. Peter also showed up that night to follow Jesus. However, he remained outside, warming himself by a fire (Fourth gospel 18:18, Mk. 14:54b & 14:67, Lu. 22:55-56). Then he denied Jesus (Fourth gospel 18:25, Mt. 26:70-74, Mk. 14:67-71, Lu. 22:57-60). After denying Jesus, Peter recalled Jesus' prophecy of this and he "went out" and "wept bitterly" (Mt. 26:75, Lu. 22:62). This all occurred before Jesus was taken to Pilate and while we are told Peter left the scene of Jesus' trial, this is never said of the "other disciple".

Nevertheless, we do need to think of both the "other disciple" and Peter as returning when they "followed Jesus" that night. This is because of some things that Jesus said earlier that evening. At one point he told his disciples, "ye shall be scattered, every man to his own, and shall leave me alone" (Fourth gospel 16:32). On the Mount of Olives a little bit later he said, "All ye shall be offended because of me this night" (Mt. 26:31, Mk. 14:27). Of course, he was correct. In Mark 14:50 we are told what happened just before Jesus was led away to the high priest. It says, "And they all forsook him and fled."

So, we should be careful not to assume that Peter and the "other disciple" did not flee the scene at Gethsemane, as did the rest of the disciples, and yet we do read that these two "followed" Jesus on that same night. Although this might appear to be a discrepancy in the scriptures, it is not.

With regard to Peter, we are told he followed Jesus "afar off" (Mt. 26:58, Mk. 14:54, Lu. 22:54). This could be an indication Peter was keeping a safe distance between himself and Jesus. On the other hand, Peter might have been following "afar off" as a result of fleeing at first, and then returning to follow, after the mob had taken Jesus away.

Is it plausible that Peter might vacillate like this? Well, after finding the courage to follow Jesus, Peter soon denied even knowing Jesus. In addition, consider Peter's vow to Jesus earlier that evening. Jesus had said, "All ye shall be offended because of me this night" (Mk. 14:27). But, Peter objected to this, and confidently singled himself out as being more reliable than the rest of the disciples. His reply was very adamant, "Although all shall be offended, yet not I" (Mk. 14:29). Jesus then responded by foretelling Peter's three denials of him that were to come later that night (Mk. 14:30). Regardless, Peter continued to insist Jesus was wrong. Mark 14:31 records Peter's rebuff of Jesus' prophecy, "But he [Peter] spake the more vehemently, If I should die with thee, I will not deny thee in any wise".

Is it reasonable to suggest Peter might have remembered his boastful words after he fled? Yes. Whatever the reason, it is clear that after he initially fled with the rest of the disciples, Peter eventually followed Jesus that night. Of course, this still leaves us with this same apparent dilemma regarding the "other disciple". Did he flee or did he follow? As you will see later, there is an answer to this seeming discrepancy for the "other disciple" also.

Courage Under Fire

When we are careful not to force the identity of John upon the text, our eyes become opened to questions about the unique character of "the disciple whom Jesus loved". Why did he behave differently (as compared to the rest of the disciples)? After the rest of the disciples fled, how was it that this man found the courage to follow Jesus? And what gave him the fortitude to stick with Jesus that night, when even Peter finally threw in the towel and left?

If Peter, James, and John couldn't even stay awake when Jesus asked them to pray, what could have motivated this "other disciple" to follow Jesus into his trial, and to stand by the cross until the care of Jesus' mother was assigned to him by Jesus?

These questions raise even more questions. Is there anyone in the Bible that we could expect to exhibit these characteristics? Does scripture give us enough evidence to explain why the "other disciple, whom Jesus loved" behaved the way he did?

As you will soon find out, the Bible is able to answer all of these questions. First though, let us remove any remaining doubts about whether or not John was "the disciple whom Jesus loved".

Chapter 4

A WRONG ASSUMPTION & MORE EVIDENCE: THE GOSPEL OF JOHN OR NOT?

"The Disciple Whom Jesus Loved" and the Last Supper

A misperception about Jesus' last Passover has tended to give credence to the idea that John could be the author of the fourth gospel. It stems from the fact that the Bible says "the disciple whom Jesus loved" was the one who "leaned on his breast at supper and said, Lord, which is he that betrayeth thee?" (Fourth gospel 21:20).

Since scripture says that Jesus "cometh with the twelve" (Mk. 14:17) and "sat down" with "the twelve" (Mt. 26:20, Lu. 22:14), many have assumed that the beloved disciple *had to be* one of "the twelve". Complicating this, there are also many Last Supper paintings that help instill an image in our mind of Jesus seated at a table with "the twelve", having a private supper with no one else in the room. These artist renditions and an erroneous assumption have led many people to accept a faulty conclusion.

Note that the Bible never says "the twelve" were the only ones present with Jesus at that event. Nowhere is it said that they dined alone, nor is there anything to indicate that Jesus' other disciples were kept away. Is there any reason to believe that Jesus and "the twelve" dined alone that last Passover? Not unless we read a constraint into the text that is not in Matthew 26:20, Mark 14:17, or Luke 22:14.

Keep in mind that it is wrong to assume that someone is not present at an event just because a passage of scripture doesn't mention him (see pg. 37; also cf. Fourth gospel 19:39-40, Mt. 26:59-60, Mk. 15:46, Lu. 23:53).

Earlier it was pointed out how it would be a mistake for us to think Peter was alone on the night he followed Jesus into the palace of the high priest simply because no one else is named in the reports of this event found in Matthew, Mark, and/or Luke. Peter was not alone when he entered the palace of the high priest that night, and yet first three gospels all omit the "other disciple" – even though he was the one who got Peter in the door! (Also, as will be shown in a moment, the testimony of Acts 1:21-22 proves "the twelve" were not the only disciples who accompanied Jesus throughout his ministry.)

There are other examples, but the point has been made. We must resist presuming too much, or building an argument from silence, lest we miss the truth. Since the gospel writers knew how to specify a limited attendance, we must not assume that those who are mentioned were the only ones at an event, unless the Bible itself specifies that restriction.

Guess Who's Coming to Dinner?

The scriptures do not state that "the twelve" were alone with Jesus the entire evening of his last Passover. The next logical question then becomes, do we find anything in the Bible implying that others might have been present? The answer is yes. There are several things that suggest this.

First off, consider that <u>Jesus and his disciples were guests in someone else's home that night</u>. Earlier that day "the disciples came to Jesus, saying unto him, Where wilt thou that we prepare for thee to eat the passover? And he said, Go into the city to such a man, and say unto him, The Master saith, My time is at hand; I will keep the passover at thy house with my disciples" (Mt. 26:17-18). What is missing is any justification for assuming the occupants of that home were supposed to vacate the premises.

Moreover, the Bible lets us know Jesus was accustomed to dining with others. The residents of those households where Jesus ate were included, not excluded. Mark 2:15 says, "as Jesus sat at meat in his [Levi's] house, many publicans and sinners sat also together with Jesus and his disciples". Also Luke 11:37 states, "a certain Pharisee besought him [Jesus] to dine with him: and he went in, and sat down to meat". We also see this when Jesus was in Bethany six days before that Passover. We are told, "There they made him a supper, and Martha served: but Lazarus was one of them that sat at the table with him" (Fourth gospel 12:2).

This suggests other questions. Who worked at that Passover supper? Scripture says Peter and John had gone earlier in the day and "made ready the passover" (Lu. 22:8-13). But, who served the food and who cleaned up? Jesus and his disciples were house guests at the time. So, isn't it likely their host took care of those details? And isn't it also probable their host would have dined with them? (Fourth gospel 12:2, Lu. 7:36, 10:38-40, 11:37 & 24:29-30 confirm this is the case.)

Since the Bible never said "the twelve" were the only people present with Jesus at that supper, why should we believe Jesus and "the twelve" spent that entire Passover evening alone by themselves?

Not Alone at the Passover

Other passages likewise indicate "the twelve" were not alone with Jesus that night. In Acts 1:21-26 a replacement for Judas was selected from a group that Peter qualified as "men which have companied with us all the time that the Lord Jesus went in and out among us, Beginning from the baptism of John, unto that same day that he was taken up from us" (Acts 1:21-22). Clearly then, **"the twelve" were not the only ones with Jesus during his earthly ministry!** This fact is rarely discussed but these words reveal that, besides "the twelve" apostles, other disciples also followed Jesus *throughout* his ministry. So, why would we conclude that they were barred from the supper if they were welcomed before and after it?

Also, in identifying his traitor Jesus said, "It is one of the twelve that dippeth with me in the dish" (Mk. 14:20). In the gospels "the twelve" is used only of those named "apostles" by Jesus (Lu. 6:13). "Disciples" refers to any of his followers, including some or all of "the twelve" (cf. Fourth gospel 6:66, Lu. 19:37). For example, following the supper we see Jesus at Gethsemane with "his disciples" (Fourth gospel 18:1). This included the apostles, minus Judas. But it surely would have also included the apostle candidates of Acts 1:21-22 and we know that the apostles were not the only ones there with Jesus, because we are told of a "young man" who was still with Jesus when all the rest had fled (Mk. 14:50-51). Immediately after the supper he was with Jesus and the disciples. Did he just show up or did he arrive with them? If he accompanied them, then he was with them earlier and that would imply he had been with them at the supper.

If "the twelve" were the <u>only</u> ones with Jesus, then why would he need to include the stipulation, "one of **the twelve**"? "The twelve" is a limiting term. If no one else was there, wouldn't Jesus have said, "one of" *you*? In fact the only other time Jesus used the term, "the twelve", he did precisely that. It was when "the twelve" affirmed their commitment after many "disciples" forsook Jesus and he responded, "Have not I chosen you twelve, and one of you is a devil?" (Fourth gospel 6:66-70). [In the Greek this reads, "you the twelve".] Thus, when he said the traitor was, "one of the twelve" – not "one of you" – it indicates <u>"the twelve" were a subset of those who were there</u>. (Moreover, Jesus used the term, "one of you" earlier at the supper (Mt. 26:21, Mk. 14:18). So when he went on to stipulate his betrayer would **be** "one of the twelve" (Mk. 14:20), that crucial detail no doubt brought relief to those disciples who were not part of "the twelve".)

Jesus also said, "with my disciples", when he sent word about who would be joining him (Mt. 26:18, Mk. 14:14, Lu. 22:11). He did not say, "the twelve" and no verse says he excluded those loyal disciples who Peter said, "companied with us all the time that the Lord Jesus went in and out among us" (Acts 1:21). But we do find both Jesus and Peter saying things that point toward others being present at the supper.

"After" the Supper?

If Jesus sat down to supper with "the twelve" and the one whom "Jesus loved" joined them later, then he wasn't one of "the twelve". The sequence of events in the fourth gospel seems to indicate that is what occurred, so we will take time to focus on this.

For example, notice how the fourth gospel's author begins his report on the events of that night, "And the supper being ended..." (Fourth gospel 13:2). Ended? Does the record in his gospel start at a later point than the other gospels do when they report on that night? As you will see, the answer is yes, but not merely by reason of this verse.

(Various Bible versions translate this verse differently because of conflicting opinions about the word tenses involved. However, instead of trying to choose between the opposing opinions of Greek scholars, let us rather look again to the Bible to see what it can tell us.)

Luke 22:17-19 tells us Jesus, "took the cup, and gave thanks, and said, Take this, and divide *it* among yourselves: For I say unto you, I will not drink of the fruit of the vine, until the kingdom of God shall come. And he took bread, and gave thanks, and brake *it*, and gave unto them, saying, This is my body which is given for you: this do in remembrance of me". Keeping this in mind, one will find that the next verse is extremely relevant to this discussion.

Luke 22:20 continues, "Likewise also the cup after supper, saying, This cup is the new testament in my blood which is shed for you". Did you catch when this occurred? It was "after supper"! [In the Greek it reads, "also the cup after having supped".] The Bible provides a confirmation of this sequence of events in First Corinthians 11:25. There we read, "also *he took* the cup when he had supped, saying this cup is the new testament in my blood". [Again the Greek says, "also the cup after having supped".]

Therefore, it can be seen that the timing of events that night (particularly what happened "after" the supper) has scriptural relevance. Next we'll learn how this pertains to the anonymous author's gospel, and see why understanding the sequence of events helps us to identify "the disciple whom Jesus loved".

Where Is the Lord's Table?

The church places great significance on the memorial custom that is referred to as Communion and/or the Lord's Table. In First Corinthians 11:26 it says, "For as often as ye eat this bread, and drink this cup, ye do shew the Lord's death till he come". Therefore, this emphasis is appropriate. Moreover, whenever Christians think about the Last Supper, the bread and the cup usually come to mind first.

The gospel accounts of that night focus on that solemn event, but only in three of the gospels. The fourth gospel makes no mention of these things! Why would the one whom "Jesus loved" have left the breaking of the bread and the sharing of the cup out of his gospel account, especially since he wrote so much about that night?

While Matthew 26:20-29, Mark 14:17-25, and Luke 22:14-38 give us the details about the supper, the fourth gospel devotes five whole chapters to the events of that night (Fourth gospel 13:3 - 17:26) — much more than the other three gospel writers combined! Yet, in spite of that, "the disciple whom Jesus loved" was the only gospel author to omit the Lord's Table. Obviously, this was not because it was unimportant. So, why is it missing?

The gospels each report different things, so the fact that this author did not include the bread and the cup is not a problem. However, his omission of this Last Supper event adds credence to the idea that he was not one of "the twelve". This event may have been left out of this author's gospel simply because he was not present when it occurred. But the Bible does not tell us why this author omitted it, so we cannot be sure. Nevertheless, this omission is understandable if the author joined Jesus and the rest of disciples after they had shared the bread and the cup – and that would also explain why his report of that evening's events begins after the supper.

This author also doesn't mention that Jesus sent two disciples to "prepare" the Passover, but the other three gospels all refer to this in varying detail, all ending with, "and they made ready the passover" (Mt. 26:17-19, Mk. 14:12-16, Lu. 22:7-13). Yet the unnamed author's omission of this item should not come as a surprise, since this omission is also consistent with an account that starts at a later point that day than the other three gospels do. Now let's look at what this author's gospel does say.

The Foot Washing Incident

After mentioning that it was in Judas' heart to betray Jesus, the very first thing that the author of the fourth gospel reports about the events of that Passover night is, amazingly, Jesus' washing of the disciples' feet. "He [Jesus] riseth from supper, and laid aside his garments; and took a towel and girded himself. After that he poured water into a basin, and began to wash the disciples' feet" (Fourth gospel 13:4-5).

Here again, the biblical record is suggesting "the supper", or at least a key part of it, had ended, since this begins with Jesus rising, "from supper". [The literal Greek reads, "he rises from the supper".] Despite this, some say they deduce just the opposite, supposing from this passage that the supper had not yet started. They infer this because they begin with the presupposition that Jesus would have done this foot washing before the meal. But, it turns out that the Bible does not support this conclusion.

For example, Luke 11:37 tells of a similar situation when a Pharisee asked Jesus to "dine with him: and he [Jesus] went in, and sat down to meat". Then the next verse notes, "And when the Pharisee saw *it*, he marveled that he had not washed before dinner" (Lu. 11:38). So keep in mind the Bible indicates that it may not have been customary for Jesus to wash before eating.

Also, in Matthew 15:2 Jesus was asked, "Why do thy disciples transgress the tradition of the elders? for they wash not their hands when they eat bread". Mark 7:5 puts it this way, "Why walk not thy disciples according to the tradition of the elders, but eat bread with unwashen hands?" So it seems that washing prior to eating was not their usual routine.

These passages imply that Jesus was not in the habit of always washing before eating, and that his disciples behaved likewise. (Similar divisions exist today. Some people learn to wash their hands before using the restroom. This differs from most Westerners, who are more accustomed to washing their hands after using the restroom.)

Given what the Bible tells us about that night, it is apparent Jesus washed the disciples' feet after the supper, not before it. Jesus may have done so, but scripture never notes where he actually washed prior to eating, hands or feet. So, while the first item recorded in this author's gospel from that Passover is the foot washing, this is still consistent with the other facts that indicate his account of that evening begins "after" the supper.

Finally, consider that after Jesus had washed the feet of his disciples, it says he, "set down again" (Fourth gospel 13:12). [The Greek says, "having reclined again".] **"Again"?** Here the author's use of the word "again" reveals Jesus had already been sitting down earlier that night – before the foot washing occurred.

"Not of You All"

The Bible tells us Jesus washed the feet of "the disciples" (this was not limited to the feet of "the twelve") (Fourth gospel 13:5). Then, after Jesus sat down again, he said, "I speak not of you all: I know whom I have chosen" (Fourth gospel 13:18). Here he contrasts a larger group, referred to as "you all", with a subset, which he called "chosen". (And we know "the twelve" were "chosen" (Fourth gospel 6:70, cf. Lu. 6:13).) However, if "the twelve" were the only ones who were present, then what distinction was Jesus making here?

Some may think these words were meant to exclude Judas Iscariot. Yet Luke 6:13 tells us Jesus, "called *unto him* his disciples: and of them he chose twelve, whom also he named apostles" and it goes on to list Judas by name (Lu. 6:16). We also find Jesus

65

saying, "Have I not chosen you twelve, and one of you is a devil?" (Fourth gospel 6:70). Therefore, we see that Judas was "chosen". So, if Judas was "chosen", who was Jesus referring to when he said, "you all"? Jesus' words here are one more indication he and "the twelve" were not alone during that supper, as here again he refers to more than just "the twelve" whom he had "chosen".

The Sequence of Last Supper Events

If "the disciple whom Jesus loved" is not required to be one of "the twelve", then the facts seem to imply the following scenario. Early that day, Jesus sent Peter and John to prepare the Passover. Later, he *arrived with* and *sat down to supper with* "the twelve". After the supper, where the account of the fourth gospel begins, Jesus got up and started to wash the feet of his disciples. When he finished washing the disciples' feet, Jesus sat down again and only then is "the disciple whom Jesus loved" introduced, sitting next to and leaning on Jesus.

The idea that the one whom "Jesus loved" must be one of "the twelve" presents irreconcilable problems (more on this later), but the key thing to realize is that this idea is not dictated by scripture. We're told that Jesus "cometh with"/"sat down" with "the twelve" (Mt. 26:20, Mk. 14:17, Lu. 22:14). Yet honest reflection forces one to admit that these verses don't limit attendance at the Last Supper to Jesus and "the twelve" – and <u>the gospel writers did know how to specify a limited attendance when that was what they actually intended to do</u> (Mt. 14:23, Mk. 5:37 & 9:8, Lu. 8:5 offer some of the many examples of this).

A Hidden Key in the Book of Acts

The next two paragraphs might initially seem unrelated to this study, but the information provided is critical to the upcoming analysis of the evidence.

Besides his betrayal of Jesus, Judas Iscariot was unique among "the twelve" for another reason. The Bible tells us Judas went to the "chief priests" to betray Jesus (Mt. 26:14-16, Mk. 14:10-11, Lu. 22:2-6). However, in addition to becoming a traitor, Judas gained another distinction at that point.

Judas' conspiracy with those "chief priests" sets him apart from "the twelve" in that those priests got to meet Judas. Nothing in the Bible specifically indicates the high priest would have known, or even recognized, any of "the twelve" other than Judas. Once you realize this, you can grasp the importance of a verse that is found in the Book of Acts. Besides the evidence that has been presented thus far, the writer of the Book of Acts recorded facts that can help us to conclusively prove the Apostle John was not the unnamed "other disciple".

Acts 4:1-23 recounts what happened to Peter and John following the healing of a crippled man. Peter and John were seized and brought before the "rulers, and elders, and scribes, and Annas the high priest, and Caiaphas..." (Acts 4:5 & 6), so they could be questioned about this miracle. If you're wondering how this helps to prove that the Apostle John was not the "other disciple", then pay close attention to the reaction of the high priest and those rulers just a few verses later.

The high priest, rulers, elders, scribes, etc. "gathered together" and began their interrogation of Peter and John (Acts 4:5-7). Peter's answer to their question is recorded in Acts 4:8-12. The very next verse describes their reaction to Peter and John.

Acts 4:13 says, speaking of the high priest and those rulers, "when they saw the boldness of Peter and John, and perceived that they were unlearned and ignorant men, they marveled; and they took knowledge of them, that they had been with Jesus".

Why did the high priest and the rest marvel? To begin with, they discovered that Peter and John "were unlearned and ignorant men" (Acts 4:13). [These two points in the Greek read, "unlettered" and "uninstructed".] Along with any Galilean accent that Peter and John may have had, it is also possible their vocabulary, clothing, and/or mannerisms would have all contributed to the idea that Peter and John lacked a formal education. Also, the Bible indicates that regional traits could be easily discerned by the people of that day (e.g., Mt. 26:73, Mk. 14:70, Lu. 22:59).

Regardless, Acts 4:13 points out what really shocked those leaders was seeing Peter and John (whom they judged to be "unlearned and ignorant") exhibit such "boldness". Instead of cowering before the educated men who would judge them, Peter and John proclaimed the truth and stood openly for the name of Jesus, charging those rulers with his death and affirming that God had raised him from the dead, while they credited Jesus with being responsible for the healing miracle that had occurred (Acts 4:9-10).

During the encounter recorded in Acts 4:5-12 those leaders were learning elementary facts about the men who were before them. Acts 4:13 also says, "they took knowledge of them [Peter and John] that they had been with Jesus". [In the Greek this reads, "they recognized them that with Jesus they were".] So, the telltale discoveries made by those rulers during this event make it clear that Peter and John were not recognized by, or familiar to, the high priest and his fellow religious leaders.

Therefore, the biblical evidence lets us know the high priest and the other rulers first became acquainted with Peter and John during that inquest. On top of this keep in mind Acts 4:6, which explicitly names both "Annas the high priest, and Caiaphas" as being among those who were present at the time.

The Apostle John and the High Priest

In the preceding section we saw the reaction of the high priest and the other religious rulers was a response to new information. It was when Acts 4 was actually happening that the high priest and the others with him learned the things which led them to conclude Peter and John: (a) were "unlearned and ignorant men", and (b) "had been with Jesus".

Here we see the high priest learning things which he would have already known if he had been previously acquainted with the two men who were standing before him. So, these facts offer conclusive proof **the high priest did not know John** (or Peter) before this encounter.

Acts 4:13 also lets us know the Apostle John cannot be the "other disciple". In order to show how this is true, we will compare Acts 4 with the record of scripture from the night Jesus was arrested and taken away to be falsely accused.

We are told Jesus was taken "to Annas first" (Fourth gospel 18:13). Then we read about two disciples that followed Jesus, "And Simon Peter followed Jesus and *so did* another disciple" (Fourth gospel 18:15). [The Greek here states, "Now there followed Jesus Simon Peter and the other disciple".] The words that follow this, however, ultimately 'clear' John, for they tell us, "that disciple was known unto the high priest". It seems that God wanted to highlight this point, for his inspired author elected to emphasize this fact by repeating it.

In the next verse we read, "Peter stood at the door without. Then went out that other disciple, which was known unto the high priest, and spake unto her that kept the door, and brought in Peter" (Fourth gospel 18:16). Therefore, there is no doubt that the "other disciple" was known to the high priest. This "other disciple" could get into the palace, and furthermore, he was responsible for getting Peter past the doorkeeper.

Consequently, **the Apostle John could not possibly have been the "other disciple" because John was not known to the high priest** (Acts 4:13). (And since both Annas and Caiaphas were present during the events of Acts 4, this holds up no matter which one was high priest during Jesus' trial.)

Prior to Acts 4:13, nothing in the Bible would suggest the Jewish leaders were acquainted with John, or were aware of his association with Jesus. In contrast to this, the "other disciple" was "known" to the high priest, who therefore would have reason to be aware of his association with Jesus prior to the night of Jesus' trial. Moreover, something was said on that night which indicates the "other disciple" was publicly associated with Jesus before that night. Yet this was not true of Peter, as the question of the doorkeeper reveals.

We are told, "the damsel that kept the door" asked Peter, "Art not thou also *one* of this man's disciples?" (Fourth gospel 18:17). The word "also" was a reference to the "other disciple" who had just talked with her (Fourth gospel 18:16). Thus, even "the damsel that kept the door" was aware the "other disciple" was associated with Jesus. But as you now know, **John's association with Jesus was not known to the high priest until Acts 4:13**.

If Not John, Then Who?

The evidence presented so far has shown the Apostle John was not the "other disciple, whom Jesus loved". Now that you are aware of the facts, you know the John tradition cannot hold up under biblical scrutiny. The truth is scripture never justified believing John was "the disciple whom Jesus loved". Also, unless one makes the assumption Jesus was alone with "the twelve" throughout his last Passover, nothing would require the one "whom Jesus loved" to even be one of "the twelve".

If "the disciple whom Jesus loved" was not the Apostle John, then who was he? The Bible can answer this question if we will search the scriptures and rely on the testimony of God's word to lead us. This is what we will begin to do now. Indeed, many facts point to the identity of this author, from proof of his relationship with Jesus, to details that suggest a possible motive for this author hiding his identity.

There is one and only one person in the Bible who can be shown to reasonably fit with **everything** scripture says about this unnamed "other disciple". As we weigh the facts that reveal the identity of the one whom "Jesus loved" it will be shown how each piece of biblical evidence concerning the author of the fourth gospel points to one very unique – and very famous – friend of Jesus.

Nevertheless recognize the case against the John idea is not dependent on the case that follows. If there is a man in jail for a crime and we uncover proof he did not do it, we do not hold him in jail until we find out who did do it. We let him go. Likewise, if biblical evidence is able to prove the "other disciple, whom Jesus loved" was not John, then we ought to admit our mistake and let go of that false tradition – whether or not we know who this person was. Still, there are some who will act as though it is okay to continue promoting the John idea so long as they object to some point in the next part of this study. But that is not okay. Whoever the one whom "Jesus loved" was, he was not John – because that tradition actually causes the Bible to contradict itself, as the testimony of God's word has already shown.

Chapter 5

THE ONE WHOM "JESUS LOVED" WAS THE AUTHOR OF THE FOURTH GOSPEL

What Is God Telling Us?

The author's explicit description of himself as "the disciple whom Jesus loved" puts the focus on Jesus' relationship to him. So, if we want to ascertain the identity of this individual, then it is logical for us to begin by searching the Bible for evidence of such a relationship in the life of Jesus. Prior to Pentecost, did Jesus have this type of relationship with anyone identified in the Bible? Yes, he did, and this was so clear that referring to this relationship was sufficient to identify one particular individual – without even mentioning his name (Fourth gospel 11:3).

Scripture never says John had this specific type of relationship with Jesus (prior to Pentecost). Moreover, being taken aside by Jesus three times with Peter and James does not say John had the unique bond implied by the designation "the disciple whom Jesus loved". As was already noted, this term lets us know this disciple was set apart from the rest of the disciples based on Jesus' relationship to him. Ironically, while this phrase has ended up being a stumbling block for so many on this author's identity, it actually is the key to identifying him!

Hidden in Plain Sight

In fact, there is so much evidence pointing to the identity of this author that one has to wonder how it could have all been overlooked. To start with, consider the term "the disciple whom Jesus loved", while it helped to hide the author's identity it also is proof of Jesus' relationship with the author.

In the gospels, do we find any man besides the unnamed author who associated with Jesus, who was also identified as being "loved" by him? Yes we do! Incredibly, two chapters before the one whom "Jesus loved" is even mentioned, the author of the fourth gospel told his readers about a friend of Jesus who was "loved" by him – in 11:3, where this message was sent to Jesus, "Lord, behold, he whom thou lovest is sick", and in 11:5, where we are told, "Jesus loved Martha, and her sister, and Lazarus".

Except for "the disciple whom Jesus loved", the **only** man who associated with Jesus who was singled out as being "loved" by Jesus was Lazarus. We are told explicitly that "Jesus loved" Lazarus. His sisters also referred to this relationship, and when "Jesus wept" prior to raising Lazarus, the Jews that were there "weeping" with his sisters attributed it to Jesus' love for him (Fourth gospel 11:19, 33 & 36). By itself the fact that "Jesus loved" him does not prove that Lazarus was the "other disciple, whom Jesus loved". However, this lead is certainly worth investigating!

Bible References to Jesus' Love

The phrase "whom Jesus loved" identifies the author as being the object of Jesus' love. Since he is not called the disciple who *loved Jesus*, this book does not examine any verses dealing with an individual's love toward Jesus. Also this study is not meant to be a discussion on the principles of love or on the general topic of the love of God. Instead, this Bible study will examine what scripture says about Jesus' love for or toward specific individuals.

Outside of the gospels, all of the references to Jesus' love are unrelated to the identity of the "other disciple". In the gospels, Jesus' love was referred to fifteen times (Fourth gospel 11:3, 5 & 36, 13:1(2x), 23 & 34, 14:21, 15:9 & 12, 19:26, 20:2, 21:7 & 20, Mk. 10:21), but **only two men** in the fourth gospel were explicitly identified as being the object of Jesus' love, Lazarus and the one whom "Jesus loved" (Fourth gospel 11:3, 5 & 36, 13:23, 19:26, 20:2, 21:7 & 20 [Forms of two Greek words, agapao and phileo, were translated "love" in these verses – and both were used to refer to 'both' men]).

The first three gospels record only one time where an individual was said to be "loved" by Jesus. Mark 10:17-22 tells us of a meeting between Jesus and an unidentified man, and this passage says that Jesus "loved him". But the passage does not state whether this person ever had any other contact with Jesus or not. So, we will proceed to take a closer look at Lazarus, since the fourth gospel noted both his association with Jesus and the fact that he was "loved" by Jesus.

A Sudden Appearance

"Lord, behold, he whom thou lovest is sick" was the appeal of Martha and Mary (Fourth gospel 11:3b), and this reveals Jesus had this relationship with Lazarus prior to that moment. This idea is confirmed two verses later when we read, "Now Jesus loved Martha, and her sister, and Lazarus" (Fourth gospel 11:5). Jesus also refers to him as, "Our friend Lazarus" (Fourth gospel 11:11b). Yet, in spite of all the history that this implies, the fourth gospel makes no mention of Lazarus until his name appears in the 11th chapter. Why is this?

Nothing in the fourth gospel overtly explains the origin of this friendship. (Still, the curious aspect of this sudden appearance is indeed parallel to what we saw regarding "the disciple whom Jesus loved".) Even more important, **the first three gospels never refer to Jesus' friendship with Lazarus or to the miracle of Jesus raising Lazarus from the dead**. (This resembles the similar omission of "the disciple whom Jesus loved" in those gospels.)

What makes this especially noteworthy is that the Bible tells of only three people who were raised from the dead by Jesus: a widow's son (Lu. 7:12-15), Jairus' daughter (Mt. 9:18-25, Mk. 5:22-24 & 35-42, Lu. 8:41-56), and Lazarus (Fourth gospel 11:14-45). The news of these astonishing events spread quickly (Fourth gospel 11:45, Mt. 9:26, Lu. 7:16-17). All were amazing miracles, but the raising of Lazarus was substantially different from the other two, as will be shown.

Jesus' Friend Becomes a Celebrity

The fact the three other gospel writers avoid any mention of the raising of Lazarus is particularly striking because of what happened *after* Lazarus was raised from the dead. "Then many of the Jews which came to Mary, and had seen the things which Jesus did, believed on him" (Fourth gospel 11:45). (Keep in mind they were eyewitnesses.) Now, compare this to what happened six days later when Jesus was again in Bethany, "Much people of the Jews therefore knew that he was there: and they came not for Jesus sake only, but that they might see Lazarus also, whom he had raised from the dead" (Fourth gospel 12:9).

So, scripture lets us know the people were attracted to Lazarus in the aftermath of this miracle. This caused such a stir "the chief priests consulted that they might put Lazarus also to death: Because that by reason of him many of the Jews went away, and believed on Jesus" (Fourth gospel 12:10-11).

Is this a testament to the allure of fame or to the witness of Lazarus or perhaps both? We lack further details as to why these people were drawn to Lazarus, but it is clear the public was aware of him and of the miracle Jesus did for him.

Consider the event people commonly call the Triumphal Entry (Fourth gospel 12:12-18). Did you know the raising of Lazarus played a key role in terms of the crowd's attendance on that day? We read of the greeting Jesus received from a cheering crowd as he rode into town on a donkey (Fourth gospel 12:12-15). Notice, however, that scripture also tells us about the crowd's motivation. Although one might assume it was the teachings of Jesus or the realization he was the Son of God that brought out the crowd on that day, the author of the fourth gospel highlighted a particular reason for the crowd's participation in that event.

This author points out the raising of Lazarus helped bring out the crowd at that Triumphal Entry. "The people therefore that was with him [Jesus] when he called Lazarus out of his grave, and raised him from the dead, bare record. For this cause the people also met him, for that they heard that he had done this miracle" (Fourth gospel 12:17-18).

Thus, the crowd's presence on that day was linked to their having heard the reports about Jesus raising Lazarus from the dead, "For this cause the people also met him" (Fourth gospel 12:18), and they had merely "heard".

The disciples of Jesus witnessed the raising of Lazarus, which was surely an electrifying and unforgettable experience! Yet, for some reason, the writers of the first three gospels decided they should not mention a word about it. What is more, we are told the formerly dead Lazarus had such an effect on the people that the priests took the extreme step of plotting to have him killed. Lazarus was **big news**. So why is it that the other gospels fail to mention any of this? If this seems odd to you, just think about how this parallels the way the first three gospels also omit "the disciple whom Jesus loved".

The Transition

Even stranger than the silence of the other gospels on all of these Lazarus matters is his abrupt disappearance from the fourth gospel. In 12:9 it tells us the people came to see Lazarus and 12:11 says he had a strong influence on the Jews. But after 12:17 refers to his return from the dead, the fourth gospel never mentions Lazarus again!

The fourth gospel's presentation of Lazarus reveals two notable facts. The first is that Lazarus is named in only eleven verses of the fourth gospel, six in chapter 11 and five in chapter 12. There is no mention of him before chapter 11 verse 1, and after chapter 12 verse 17 he seems to vanish.

But what is even more interesting to note is this <u>friend whom "Jesus loved"</u> is last mentioned in chapter 12 – just before the obscure and unnamed <u>disciple whom "Jesus loved"</u> is first mentioned in the very next chapter (Fourth gospel 13:23).

If you are inclined to think that this transition might be simply an unimportant coincidence, then just wait, for there is much more evidence to come.

Still, one has to admit this presents us with a striking parallel. The one man associated with Jesus who was also singled out as being "loved" by Jesus **abruptly vanishes** from the text, and then the only disciple to be singled out as being "loved" by Jesus **abruptly appears** in this same gospel.

The sequence of these things in the Bible is no accident! Furthermore, this newly evident disciple plays an important role in the events that follow.

Some may want to dispute the thesis that the "other disciple, whom Jesus loved" was Lazarus because it might seem inconsistent for him to hide his identity as author of the gospel while mentioning his name several times in the same book. However, as will be shown a little later, by comparing scripture with scripture one is able to grasp a perfectly logical and biblically sound reason as to why Lazarus may have done precisely that.

Others may point out the Bible does not call Lazarus a "disciple" and we will also deal with this potential difficulty.

For now, though, let us look at the second reason why the order of these events is significant. As noted above, this author did not employ the term "the disciple whom Jesus loved" until after Lazarus is raised from the dead in the text and that miracle was certainly a powerful act of love toward Lazarus. During his earthly ministry Jesus did not eliminate suffering and death for everyone and the Bible tells of only three people Jesus raised from the dead while he was here. Lazarus was definitely privileged in this regard. This is also extremely relevant to the sequence of gospel events because **after Lazarus was raised from the dead he would never be and could never be the same again.**

Dead Man Walking

The raising of Lazarus is no fairy tale. It is not fiction. It was an important event in history. So, let's take the time to consider the reality of this situation. Lazarus had a close relationship with Jesus *before* he was raised from the dead. Their relationship was close enough that when he was sick, his sisters sent for Jesus with the message, "Lord, behold, he whom thou lovest is sick" (Fourth gospel 11:3). We are not told about this relationship but it must have existed for some time, and the message reveals his sisters felt that "he whom thou lovest" applied to Lazarus, as their message didn't even mention his name.

Given that Lazarus had a close relationship with Jesus before Jesus raised him from the dead, what do you think that relationship would have been like after that experience? How would Lazarus have been changed by that one-of-a-kind gift from God?

Is it reasonable to believe that Lazarus simply said 'Thanks, Jesus!' and went back to his usual, daily routine – spending his time on the cares of this world, just like his fellow citizens?

It would be laughable to think Lazarus could have just brushed off the tomb dust and returned to his normal life. Pause and take time to consider that miracle. It would surely be the most profound event in anyone's life. But for one who was already close to Jesus the effect of this miracle must have been extremely transforming. How would Lazarus have been different after that?

Later, when Jesus came to Bethany again, "they made him a supper" (Fourth gospel 12:1-2). Yet no one would believe that "a supper" was the full extent of Lazarus' effort to show his gratitude or his loyalty.

Peter once said, "Lord, to whom shall we go? thou hast the words of eternal life" (Fourth gospel 6:68). Where would Lazarus have gone? He had not only heard the words of Jesus, he had experienced their power firsthand, in a way that few ever did. In light of this, which of the following is most likely?

A. Lazarus lived in fear of death for the rest of his time on earth, because he knew what it was like to die and dreaded having to do it again.
B. Lazarus returned to what he was doing before he got sick. He remained a normal guy, tried to be a good person, observed the Sabbath, etc.
C. Lazarus was thoroughly and radically changed in response to that rare and precious gift from God.

Like White on Rice!

If we take the time to think upon these things we realize that, since Lazarus already had a special relationship with Jesus, his response to that gift from God would not have been limited to mere gratitude. Without a doubt, he would have been motivated to be even closer and more loyal to his friend Jesus than he had previously been.

In fact, from that day forward, Lazarus, more than anyone else, would have reason to stick close to Jesus – 'Like white on rice!', as the old saying goes. Also, not surprisingly, close to Jesus is exactly where we next find Lazarus.

When Jesus was in Bethany again, we read, "There they made him a supper, and Martha served: but Lazarus was one of them that sat at the table with him" (Fourth gospel 12:2). This verse and 11:44 are the only verses that actually depict Lazarus, so this is the last time that Lazarus is depicted in the Bible. (Lazarus is later mentioned in 12:9, 10, and 17, but he is not depicted as being present.) Since this is his last appearance, what stands out about this verse?

Where we find Lazarus in his final explicit appearance is the key thing to note. The <u>last</u> time that Lazarus is seen he is **sitting with Jesus at a supper table** and the <u>first</u> time that the one whom "Jesus loved" is seen he is **leaning on Jesus at a supper table** (Fourth gospel 12:2 & 13:23).

Is this simply another remarkable coincidence or is it part of a larger pattern of evidence?

You will have to decide, but for now let us look at another occasion when someone seemed to stick close to Jesus. The night Jesus was arrested, the "other disciple" followed Jesus and "went in with Jesus into the palace of the high priest" (Fourth gospel 18:15). Later, when Jesus was on the cross, he looked down and "saw his mother, and the disciple standing by, whom he loved" (Fourth gospel 19:26). We do not find "the twelve" standing at the foot of the cross, yet **this** disciple was there. Why him and not the rest? What gave this disciple the courage and stamina to stick with Jesus until he was assigned to the mother of Jesus and "took her unto his own *home*"?

The evening prior, Peter, James, and John let Jesus down by falling asleep three times. Then, the disciples fled when Jesus was seized. Peter and the "other disciple" reappeared and followed Jesus. But, while this "other disciple" went "in with Jesus", Peter stayed out by the fire, denied knowing Jesus, and soon left. By contrast, as Jesus was on the cross, the disciple "whom he loved" was close enough for the crucified Jesus to speak to him. So, why did this beloved disciple behave in a way that set him apart as being a cut above the rest of the disciples?

Been There. Done That.

Given their relationship, Lazarus must have known about Jesus' many miracles. Then, on top of hearing about or perhaps even seeing miracles, Lazarus personally experienced coming back from the dead. What priority would Lazarus have put on self-preservation after he was raised?

Survival is a very potent human instinct, but it is still fairly easy to grasp why the raised Lazarus might <u>not</u> have behaved like the rest of the disciples. God taught him, in the most emphatic way possible, that death isn't necessarily final and, more important, that Jesus could give life. Thereafter, faith in Jesus would not have been just a mental concept for him. He had become living proof of the power of Jesus, and every time he awoke, he was likely to recall the moment of that miracle.

Regarding death, Lazarus had 'Been there. Done that.', though he would surely not have been cavalier about it. Imagine the effect this miracle had on his life. Such an experience could reasonably be expected to have had a significant effect on his fear of death. (Possibly even overcome it?)

The Courage Evidence

A close call with death can cause a person to change drastically. Being dead for four days, along with his interactions with those who came to see him after his return (Fourth gospel 12:9 & 17), would've given Lazarus a **wholly unique** outlook on life. Could this lead to the type of courage and character the Bible attributes to the unnamed "other disciple"?

The "other disciple" went "with Jesus into the palace of the high priest", and we have seen that he was a known associate of Jesus (Fourth gospel 18:15-17). Unlike the rest of the disciples, he didn't act in a way that exhibited a concern for preserving his own life. Nevertheless, this is perfectly understandable if this individual was Lazarus.

Also, if the "other disciple" was Lazarus, then he was truly at risk when he entered the "palace of the high priest", because the "chief priests" wanted to kill Lazarus too (Fourth gospel 12:10). We are not told if Lazarus knew about the plot to kill him at that time or if he learned about it at a later point. Regardless, the unique behavior of the "other disciple" still befits a raised-from-the-dead Lazarus (i.e., one who would stick with Jesus even when his own life was at risk). Some may ask, 'If the "other disciple" was Lazarus, then why didn't they kill him that night?' Well, they had planned to kill Lazarus because he had caused people to believe on Jesus. So if they killed Jesus, which they were in the process of doing, then they had no reason to bother with Lazarus. But the Bible does not speak to this, so we cannot be totally sure.

What Is a Disciple?

Some may try to argue against the theory the "other disciple" was Lazarus by pointing out he was not called a "disciple" in scripture. This is true, but that does not mean he was not a disciple. It is clear he was a friend of Jesus and the apostles, for Jesus referred to him as, "Our friend Lazarus" (Fourth gospel 11:11). So Lazarus must have spent time with them. However, the question for us is: Would it be correct to refer to Lazarus as a "disciple"?

"Disciple" was not a rank like Eagle Scout. One didn't pass a test to become a "disciple". In the Bible, disciples come and disciples go (cf. Fourth gospel 6:66, Acts 6:1). This term is used in numerous verses, about a wide variety of people. [In the Greek this word simply means a "learner" or "pupil".]

While it is not precisely clear what made one a "disciple", to contend Lazarus was not a "disciple" merely because he is not explicitly called a "disciple" is unreasonable in light of what we know about his appearances in the Bible. The reason the first three gospels do not call Lazarus a "disciple" is simple, **they never mention him at all** – not his friendship with Jesus, not even the miracle of his being raised from the dead. The one gospel that tells us about Lazarus also does not call him a "disciple", but this would fit with Lazarus using the term "the disciple whom Jesus loved" to cloak his identity as author of this gospel. (Another possibility is Lazarus may have graduated from friend to dedicated follower of Jesus only in the aftermath of what Jesus did for him and, if so, that may be why the author referred to himself as a "disciple" only after he reported that miracle.)

The author wrote, "these are written, that ye might believe that Jesus is the Christ, the Son of God" (Fourth gospel 20:31). We will revisit this verse later when we discuss his motive for hiding his identity. For now though, let us realize the author was only including things that he believed would accomplish this goal. As we will see, this was reason enough for him not to call Lazarus a "disciple". (Not identifying Lazarus as a "disciple" may well be the key reason the author's effort at anonymity was so effective.)

Finally, to suppose Lazarus never became a "disciple" is not reasonable. We know he was "loved" by Jesus. He was raised from the dead by Jesus. He had supper with Jesus. Is it fair then to infer that Lazarus would have *learned* from his experiences and his relationship with Jesus? Yes, it is.

The Character Evidence

Coming back from the dead would certainly affect one's character. Thus, it is reasonable to think that Lazarus might exhibit a high degree of courage and unusual faithfulness toward Jesus, in a way that would set him apart from "the twelve" and the rest of the disciples. Do we see Lazarus behaving this way? Well, if Lazarus was the "other disciple", then surely he did manifest these traits. So, we will consider the actions of the "other disciple" to see if he behaved like a raised-from-the-dead Lazarus would act.

Notice how the one whom "Jesus loved" was set apart from the rest of the disciples by his reaction on the night of the supper. The topic of the betrayer came up several times that evening. First, before the bread and the cup, when Jesus said the traitor was "one of you" (Mt. 26:21b, Mk. 14:18b), the disciples were "sorrowful, and began every one of them to say unto him, Lord, is it I?" (Mt. 26:22; cf. Mk. 14:19). That isn't the same as 'Who is it?', since to ask the question was to doubt their own character! Yet, that ended when Jesus ruled out all but "the twelve" by saying, "*It is* one of the twelve that dippeth with me in the dish" (Mk. 14:20). Then, after the bread and the cup, the issue came up again. But Jesus had already ruled out all but "the twelve", so this time the response takes the form of a dispute about which apostle it would be, "they began to enquire among themselves, which of **them** it was that should do this thing" (Lu. 22:23).

Still, the reaction of one person did stand out from the rest, and we see this later that evening, after the foot washing, when Jesus sat down "again"

(Fourth gospel 13:12). At that point, he once again raised the issue of the traitor (Fourth gospel 13:21), and it says, "then the disciples looked one on another, doubting of whom he spake" (Fourth gospel 13:22). Peter then took a step to probe further, just not directly. "Now there was leaning on Jesus' bosom one of his disciples, whom Jesus loved. Simon Peter therefore beckoned to him, that he should ask who it should be of whom he [Jesus] spake" (Fourth gospel 13:23-24).

Why didn't Peter ask his own question? Was he one of those who had doubted their own loyalty? Peter was an apostle but he still chose to go through the one whom "Jesus loved" to ask this question. What was there about this disciple that made Peter turn to <u>him</u>, instead of just asking Jesus directly? (Would Peter have gone through John to ask Jesus a question? Mark 10:41 suggests that he would not.)

Anyone at the table was close enough to ask Jesus a question, yet Peter chose to prompt the one whom "Jesus loved" to do it. In any case, when Peter signaled him to ask which one of "the twelve" would be the traitor, he didn't hesitate or exhibit self-doubt like the rest had. "He then lying on Jesus' breast saith unto him, Lord, who is it?" (Fourth gospel 13:24-25). Indeed, his ease in posing the question befits the raised "friend" whom "Jesus loved", since Lazarus would have known whoever the betrayer would be, it could not be him! We see that the one whom "Jesus loved" did not ask, 'Is it I?' Unlike Peter, he appears to have no qualms about asking Jesus the question. He seems sure of himself and his physical position even suggests this, for the author tells us that he was leaning on Jesus.

Three times the author describes his position at this event (Fourth gospel 13:23 & 25, 21:20). This wasn't just to record the seating arrangements. His position at the table that night gives us insight into how close he was to Jesus personally. He could lean on Jesus because they had a close relationship. No one else is said to have "leaned" on Jesus. This bond did not materialize out of thin air on that night, and it seems to be different from the bond that Jesus had with the rest of his disciples, including Peter. The quality and degree of camaraderie that is revealed in this action imply a secure friendship and an obvious devotion.

Regardless, the fact is that Peter's choice to use the one whom "Jesus loved" to ask about the betrayer tells us that he was not one of "the twelve", for surely Peter would not have tagged any of the apostles to ask this question – because Jesus had already said that one of <u>them</u> would be the traitor (Mk. 14:20). One of the apostles could not be trusted and Peter wanted to know who it was. If he was going to get someone to ask for him, it would have been someone who was **not** one of "the twelve".

Does the Evidence Fit?

Is it reasonable to suppose that Lazarus may have been privileged to enjoy an especially close friendship with Jesus at the time of this event? Yes, it is. Would such a relationship help explain some of the actions of the one "whom Jesus loved" on the night of the supper? Does the evidence fit Lazarus? If you have not yet been persuaded, then perhaps the evidence from the morning that Jesus' vacant tomb was discovered will convince you.

Resurrection Morning

Take a close look at the unnamed author's account of events on resurrection morning. It is not just a confirmation of the vacant tomb. If that was all God wanted, then the author might well have been inspired to use fewer words. So, keep an eye out for the details that his words contain, because they can actually provide us with quite a bit of revealing data regarding the "other disciple" (and **all** of it ends up supporting the case for Lazarus).

"The first *day* of the week cometh Mary Magdalene early, when it was yet dark, unto the sepulchre, and seeth the stone taken away from the sepulchre. Then she runneth, and cometh to Simon Peter, and to the other disciple, whom Jesus loved, and saith unto them, They have taken away the Lord out of the sepulchre, and we know not where they have laid him. Peter therefore went forth, and that other disciple, and came to the sepulchre. So they ran both together: and the other disciple did outrun Peter, and came first to the sepulchre" (Fourth gospel 20:1-4).

Pause for a moment and consider that last sentence. Of course, it's possible the author wanted to record this fact merely in order to tell us that he (the "other disciple") was the better athlete. Or perhaps the author was simply being accurate. There is, however, another possibility that we should consider. Ask yourself: Other than sheer athletic ability, what could have caused the "other disciple" to "outrun Peter"? (The answer to this, it turns out, also suggests why this point was even noteworthy.)

The answer is adrenaline. The "other disciple" might well have outrun Peter simply because he had a more intense desire to see that tomb. If so, then he would have pushed himself harder to get there more quickly. As you consider this, remember that it was the one whom "Jesus loved" who wrote this and took the time to describe this seemingly trivial detail from that day. Also, note it is highly likely the idea that Jesus' body was not in the tomb would have had a special impact on Lazarus – who had recently vacated a tomb of his own.

Now, let's pick up where we left off. "And he [the "other disciple"] stooping down, *and looking in*, saw the linen clothes lying; yet went he not in. Then cometh Simon Peter following him, and went into the sepulchre, and seeth the linen clothes lie, And the napkin, that was about his head, not lying with the linen clothes, but wrapped together in a place by itself. Then went in also that other disciple, which came first to the sepulchre, and he saw, and believed. For as yet they knew not the scripture, that he must rise again from the dead" (Fourth gospel 20:5-9).

In our day 'the witness of the empty tomb' is a term used by those who say the empty tomb itself is proof of Jesus' resurrection. While it may be well intentioned, this is not strictly biblical. First, realize that the things Peter and the "other disciple" saw in the tomb that morning did not harmonize with their understanding of scripture. We know this because we read, "as yet they knew not the scripture, that he [Jesus] must rise again from the dead" (Fourth gospel 20:9). This point is particularly significant because <u>these two men react differently</u>.

In addition, notice the Bible makes it clear **the tomb was not empty.** Even though the tomb no longer contained the body of Jesus, it did contain some very important pieces of evidence.

The Evidence Inside the Tomb

Mary Magdalene told Peter and the "other disciple" that the body of Jesus had been removed, which prompted them to rush to the tomb. It says, "So they ran both together: and the other disciple did outrun Peter, and came first to the sepulchre". When the "other disciple" got there he stooped down and "saw the linen clothes" lying inside, at which point he stopped and "went he not in". When Peter got there, however, he did not stop. He went right in. The "other disciple" was outside until that point, but "then" he "went in also" (cf. Fourth gospel 20:2, 4, 5, 6 & 8).

Why do you think the "other disciple" stopped when he "saw the linen clothes"? After Peter went in, the "other disciple" did too. Why didn't he go in when he arrived? He ran, so he must have felt a sense of urgency. Despite this, he seems to freeze just outside the entrance until Peter passes by him and enters the tomb. So, why did the sight of "the linen clothes" cause him to stop in his tracks?

In a moment you will see there is a reason why this curious behavior of the "other disciple" is further evidence that he was Lazarus. But first let us look at the difference in the reactions of Peter and the "other disciple" to the items they saw in the tomb on that morning – **one of them "believed"**!

"Then went in also that other disciple, which came first to the sepulchre, and he saw, and believed" (Fourth gospel 20:8). The "other disciple" was the one who believed, but notice when this occurred. It happened only after he entered the tomb and saw "the napkin, that was about his [Jesus'] head, not lying with the linen clothes, but wrapped together in a place by itself" (Fourth gospel 20:7).

The First Disciple to Believe

When he witnessed those "linen clothes" and "the napkin that was about his [Jesus'] head" in the tomb, the "other disciple" suddenly "believed". Why? The author takes the time to depict these items precisely, and he underscores the "linen clothes" by repeating this phrase three times (Fourth gospel 20:5-7). This is important. We can learn something about this author/"other disciple, whom Jesus loved" from the emphasis that he placed on these things and the effect that they had on him, "he saw, and believed".

This is the first time the word "believed" is used after the resurrection and it pertains to the "other disciple"! This is no small point. His being the first person who "believed" is extremely significant. (The Appendix will expound on this point later.)

Does scripture indicate the Apostle John had any reason to react in a unique way to those items that were in the tomb? No, it does not. Furthermore, note the Bible does not state that Peter "believed" (at that point in time). The author here makes it clear the vacant tomb, "the linen clothes", and "the napkin" did not have the same impact on Peter.

However, the sight of "the linen clothes" likely would have stopped Lazarus in his tracks and the sight of "the napkin" would have had a unique effect on him. The significance of these items would not have been lost on Lazarus, for he had experienced waking up after he had been dressed him in "linen", the material that was used to wrap dead bodies!

The "Linen" Effect

"And he [Lazarus] that was dead came forth, bound hand and foot with graveclothes: and his face was bound about with a napkin" (Fourth gospel 11:44). It's no accident that the author took the time to mention the seemingly trivial detail of the "napkin" with regard to Lazarus also. Moreover, it was only after the sight of the "napkin" that the "other disciple" reacted – **then** "he saw, and believed".

While the author did not report what Lazarus' "graveclothes" were made of, he noted that the Jews used "linen" to bury the bodies in those days, "Then they took the body of Jesus, and wound it in linen clothes with the spices, as the manner of the Jews is to bury" (Fourth gospel 19:40). So, this would indicate that "linen" was likely used for Lazarus' body also.

Let's take a quick look at the usage of "linen" in the New Testament. The English word "linen" was used to translate several different Greek words, but only two of these Greek words involve dead bodies. These two words were both used to describe the material that covered the body of Jesus, so they may well be synonyms (cf. Fourth gospel 19:40 compared to Mt. 27:59; and Lu. 23:53 compared to Lu. 24:12).

One of these words always refers to the cloth covering a corpse. Likewise, the other always refers to the cloth covering a corpse, with one exception. We'll discuss this curious exception a little bit later. What we need to think about at this juncture is how Lazarus would have reacted to the sight of the items which had been covering the body of Jesus.

What was the first thing Lazarus saw when he came back from the dead? Significantly, it would have been the "napkin" that covered his own face! In the moments after Jesus called him back to life, Lazarus came out of his cave-grave still wrapped in his graveclothes and Jesus gave the instruction, "Loose him, and let him go" (Fourth gospel 11:44).

It is unlikely Lazarus ever forgot being loosed. Therefore, it is logical to suggest that **the sight of Jesus' abandoned graveclothes would have had a powerful and wholly unique effect on Lazarus**.

The "other disciple" ran to Jesus' tomb and stooped down to go in, but instead he stopped when he saw "the linen clothes" (Fourth gospel 20:3-5). When he did go in moments later, this "other disciple" became the first person to believe on the risen Lord, "he saw, and believed" (Fourth gospel 20:8).

In light of this evidence, particularly given his reactions to "the linen clothes" and "the napkin", can we conclude that the behavior of the "other disciple" would befit Lazarus? The facts that were recorded about this event fit together logically and completely if the "other disciple" was Lazarus.

The Fishing Trip

After resurrection morning "the disciple whom Jesus loved" is next seen when he and five others volunteer to accompany Peter, who announced that he was going fishing. "There were together Simon Peter, and Thomas called Didymus, and Nathanael of Cana in Galilee, and the *sons of* Zebedee, and two other of his disciples. Simon Peter saith unto them, I go a fishing. They say unto him, We also go with thee" (Fourth gospel 21:2-3a). They caught nothing that night, and the next morning "Jesus stood on the shore: but the disciples knew not that it was Jesus" (Fourth gospel 21:3b-4). He spoke with them and said to, "Cast the net on the right side of the ship", and when they did they could not pull in the net because of "the multitude of fishes" (Fourth gospel 21:5-6). In the next verse the author's presence is revealed when we read, "Therefore that disciple whom Jesus loved saith unto Peter, It is the Lord" (Fourth gospel 21:7).

So we see "the disciple whom Jesus loved" was the first disciple to recognize Jesus that day. More important, however, is the author's list of who was in attendance, for right after he mentioned "the *sons of* Zebedee" (James and John), he noted that two unnamed disciples were present. This reference to an unnamed disciple fits with the author's pattern of concealing his identity at this point in his gospel. Still, it should grab our attention when we see that the author **grouped John in with the five apostles** whom he chose to identify in the first part of his list; but then, in contrast with that set of apostle names, he lumped together the two unnamed disciples and tacked them on to the end of his list (Fourth gospel 21:2).

The author listed "the *sons of* Zebedee" with the apostles, yet he referred to himself anonymously (as "that disciple whom Jesus loved") moments later in verse 7 – and this argues against his being John. The author consistently used anonymous terms to refer to himself since he first did so in his record of Jesus' last Passover, and he continued that practice in this very passage. So, it would be totally contrary to that effort for the author to have included himself with the group he elected to name in verse 2.

The First Error

Later during that event, the disciples came to shore and dined with Jesus (Fourth gospel 21:7-14). Following that, Jesus had a conversation with Peter (Fourth gospel 21:15-19). Immediately thereafter we read, "Then Peter, turning about, seeth the disciple whom Jesus loved following, which also leaned on his breast at supper, and said, Lord, which is he that betrayeth thee? Peter seeing him saith to Jesus, Lord, and what *shall* this man *do*?" (Fourth gospel 21:20-21). To this Jesus replied, "If I will that he tarry till I come, what *is that* to thee? follow thou me" (Fourth gospel 21:22).

Next, there is a very strange reference to the unnamed disciple. "Then went this saying abroad among the brethren, that that disciple should not die: yet Jesus said not unto him, He shall not die; but If I will that he tarry till I come, what *is that* to thee?" (Fourth gospel 21:23). Here the author reports, and seeks to correct, an error that had been circulating "among the brethren". So, the first error about this disciple occurred long before he was mistakenly called John, when some were falsely taught that he wouldn't die!

How should one respond to a false teaching? The method used by this God-inspired author was to note what was not said and to emphasize what was **actually** said. He pointed out that Jesus did not say what the rumor said ("He shall not die"), and then he again quoted Jesus' words verbatim ("If I will that he tarry till I come, what *is that* to thee?"). This author offered no further commentary on Jesus' words, but rather chose simply to bear witness to the words of Jesus and let them speak for themselves.

The author clearly expected that his readers could understand the words of Jesus. But if those words were sufficient for the readers of his gospel, why were they misinterpreted by those who spread the false notion that this author would "not die"?

A Telltale Rumor

The fourth gospel's author tried to correct the misunderstanding that had been circulating among "the brethren". We are not told if Jesus' words were misinterpreted by one or more of the men that were on the fishing trip, or if the "not die" idea sprang up later, after others had been told about this trip. But regardless of who started the rumor, the fact is that the brethren accepted the notion that the one whom "Jesus loved" would "not die". This begs the question, What could have caused this? The words spoken by Jesus on that day did not dictate such a conclusion, for the author twice quoted Jesus' words verbatim (Fourth gospel 21:22 & 23). So he knew the "not die" idea did not correspond to the words of Jesus but, rather, it was wrongly *substituted for* his words.

There is a difference between those who had heard Jesus' words recounted by the men who were on the fishing trip and those who would later read those words in this author's book. The former group would have had a key piece of information that the author withheld from his readers, and interestingly, this would help to explain why the "not die" idea was ever believed in the first place. The knowledge of the identity of "the disciple whom Jesus loved" is what differentiates these two groups.

The author's identity was concealed from the readers of his gospel. The disciples of Jesus, on the other hand, knew "the disciple whom Jesus loved". His identity was not a mystery to them and, initially at least, they would have included this information in their testimony of what happened on the fishing trip.

What was it about this particular disciple that caused some to jump to the wrong conclusion and led them to assume that they could interpret Jesus' words, "If I will that he tarry till I come" as meaning, "that disciple should not die"?

The erroneous idea that he "should not die" was not caused by what Jesus said. Rather, it arose because of whom Jesus had been talking about!

What if the men on the fishing trip, and those who heard about this event, knew that Jesus' words referred to Lazarus? Since he had already died and been brought back from the dead, a reason for the erroneous rumor becomes evident. One can see why some of them might jump to the conclusion that Jesus' words meant, "he should not die".

Jesus had displayed his willingness to have his "friend" Lazarus loosed from the bonds of death, even after four days (and that miracle took place not all that long before this misunderstanding occurred). This was a very special blessing, one not granted to all of Jesus' disciples, nor their families and friends. Lazarus was one of the few individuals who had ever been chosen to receive this one-of-a-kind gift and 'everyone' knew it (Fourth gospel 12:9, 11 & 18).

If the one whom "Jesus loved" was Lazarus, then, as noted, there is a logical explanation for the origin of the false rumor. Since Jesus had already raised his friend Lazarus from the dead, those who knew that Lazarus was the subject of Jesus' words had mistakenly inferred he would be exempted from having to undergo a second physical death.

The "not die" rumor may also have arisen due to people reading a false meaning into these words – "he that believeth in me, though he were dead, yet shall he live: And whosoever liveth and believeth in me shall never die" (Fourth gospel 11:25-26). Jesus said this to Martha in the context of his raising of Lazarus and she likely mentioned this when she talked about that event. So, the "not die" idea could also be linked to a misapplication of Jesus' words "shall never die".

Once again, it turns out the facts surrounding this disciple perfectly fit Lazarus. This telltale rumor easily harmonizes with all of the other biblical data, if Lazarus was the one whom "Jesus loved". We will be considering still more evidence in support of this conclusion but first let us try to answer this question: Why did this author conceal his identity?

Chapter 6

WHY DID THE AUTHOR WRITE THE GOSPEL? & MORE EVIDENCE OF HIS IDENTITY

The Motive?

The fourth gospel's anonymous author took the time to record his purpose for writing his book, and that purpose may be linked to the reason that he hid his identity. He wrote, "And many other signs truly did Jesus in the presence of his disciples, which are not written in this book: But these are written, that ye might believe that Jesus is the Christ, the Son of God, and that believing ye might have life through his name" (Fourth gospel 20:30-31).

The author's intent, therefore, was to focus the attention of his readers on Jesus and to provide information that would help them to "believe that Jesus is the Christ, the Son of God". While this may appear to be merely the author's goal for his gospel, it turns out that this objective also provided a motive for this author to cloak his identity. (All of this was under the inspiration of God, of course, but God does use individuals in their existing circumstances to declare His will and carry it out.)

As the author's intent was to point people to Jesus, he would have avoided doing anything that might have interfered with that goal. Also, there is evidence Lazarus would have had reason to believe his identity could have interfered with that objective. If we think about what happened after Lazarus was raised from the dead, then we can understand the problem that Lazarus had to face; he had become a 'celebrity'. If he was the author of the fourth gospel, this may have presented a dilemma for Lazarus, in the form of a potential conflict with that stated goal.

The Fame Problem

In chapter 12, which is the last place that the author mentions Lazarus, we get a feel for just how famous he became. For instance, it says, "they came not for Jesus' sake only, but that they might see Lazarus also, whom he had raised from the dead" (Fourth gospel 12:9). Consider the implications of that – **"they came not for Jesus' sake only"**! How do you think that would have affected Lazarus? Would he have enjoyed the spotlight and basked in the glory that this brought to him? There is no evidence that Jesus' "friend" Lazarus took advantage of this situation or milked it for his own ego. (Actually, the sudden disappearance of Lazarus from the pages of the fourth gospel indicates quite the contrary.)

Prior to Pentecost we do not read of people wanting to see Peter or any of the apostles "also", even though they helped feed the crowds (Mt. 14:19, 15:36, etc.), and displayed power over "devils" (Lu. 10:17). The focus of the people had always been Jesus. They came to confront, see, touch, listen to, or be healed by Jesus. But after Lazarus was raised from the dead in front of many eyewitnesses, the people came to see him "also". Therefore, the "friend" whom "Jesus loved" faced a peculiar dilemma.

We read, "by reason of him [Lazarus] many of the Jews went away, and believed on Jesus" (Fourth gospel 12:11). Moreover, the raising of Lazarus was a key reason that the crowd met Jesus when he rode in to Jerusalem on a donkey. "For this cause the people also met him [Jesus], for they heard that he had done this miracle" (Fourth gospel 12:18).

This may lead some to suggest that Lazarus' new found fame was a good thing, because it could help to draw more people, who would then get to hear Jesus speak. However, there is good reason to suspect that this would not have achieved a lasting result, since the crowd at that Triumphal Entry was not cheering for Jesus just a few days later, when the choice for pardon was Jesus or Barabbas.

There is no reason to believe that the raised Lazarus was anything but loyal to his friend Jesus. Nevertheless, he became a novelty that people also sought in addition to Jesus (Fourth gospel 12:9).

We should immediately recognize this would have presented Lazarus with an unusual problem. John the Baptist articulated the idea, "He [Jesus] must increase, but I *must* decrease" (Fourth gospel 3:30). One obvious way Lazarus could avoid drawing any attention away from Jesus would be to 'disappear' (by obscuring his identity or becoming anonymous).

The fourth gospel's author explicitly said he did not report everything Jesus did (Fourth gospel 20:30). His book sought to achieve a stated goal – that its readers, "might believe that Jesus is the Christ, the Son of God" and that they would, "have life through his name" (Fourth gospel 20:31). The author had a reason for cloaking his identity. If he was Lazarus, then he may have hidden his identity to prevent his notoriety from interfering with the stated goal of the gospel. Is this in fact what led the author to hide his identity? While we cannot know for sure, this explanation is at least a reasonable and biblically sound possibility.

What about Him?

Even the disciples were not immune to the distraction effect, as can be seen when six of them accompanied Peter on a fishing trip and Jesus paid them a visit. While seven disciples were present, the resurrected Jesus took the time to focus on Peter (Fourth gospel 21:15-19). Moreover, we are also told that this was only, "the third time that Jesus shewed himself to his disciples, after that he was risen from the dead" (Fourth gospel 21:14).

However, in spite of Jesus' focus on him, it seems as if Peter's attention was easily distracted – by the presence of "the disciple whom Jesus loved"! "Then Peter, turning about seeth the disciple whom Jesus loved following; which also leaned on his breast at supper and said, Lord, which is he that betrayeth thee? Peter seeing him saith to Jesus, Lord, and what *shall* this man *do*?" (Fourth gospel 21:20-21).

Instead of responding to the words that Jesus had just spoken to him, Peter appears to change the subject. It's not likely that he did this simply because "the disciple whom Jesus loved" happened to fall in his line of sight. So, what do you think could have prompted Peter to ask this question?

Furthermore, several disciples were present, so what motivated Peter to focus on "the disciple whom Jesus loved"? Verses 20 and 21 do refer to him "following" and Peter's "seeing him", but the mere fact that he was nearby would not have been a sufficient reason for Peter to single out this one particular disciple from the rest who were there.

At that instant, Peter deliberately referred to this one disciple only. Why? Well let us consider the possibility Peter may have asked specifically about "the disciple whom Jesus loved" at that moment **because of who this disciple was** – since Peter would have known this man as Lazarus!

One other thing to take into account is the point at which Peter's attention turned to the one whom "Jesus loved". This is noteworthy because the topic of conversation had just changed, and at that moment Jesus was speaking about Peter's death!

Jesus Foretells Peter's Death

"This spake he [Jesus] signifying by what death he [Peter] should glorify God" (Fourth gospel 21:19). Without getting into the particulars of Jesus' words in verse 18, note that we're told that he raised the topic of Peter's death. Then Jesus had two more words for Peter, "Follow me" (Fourth gospel 21:19).

When the matter of his death was raised, Peter seemed to change the subject, which might be dismissed by some as a typical reaction to anxiety. But bear in mind that the one speaking to Peter was the resurrected Jesus, who had overcome death.

When Jesus told Peter, "by what death he should glorify God" what did Peter do? "Then Peter, turning about, seeth the disciple whom Jesus loved... Peter seeing him saith to Jesus, Lord, and what *shall* this man *do*?" (Fourth gospel 21:20-21). [The literal Greek reads, "Lord, but of this one what".]

Why, upon learning "by what death he should glorify God", did Peter feel compelled to refer to one particular disciple? Was Peter merely concerned for this disciple or is there a more rational explanation that might better account for his question?

Of course, if the one whom "Jesus loved" was Lazarus, then we can see logic in Peter's question. Peter knew Lazarus had been raised from the dead, so he may have been asking if Lazarus would have to die again – especially since he likely heard Jesus say, "he that believeth in me, though he were dead, yet shall he live: And whosoever liveth and believeth in me shall never die" prior to raising Lazarus (Fourth gospel 11:25-26). But regardless of why Peter asked his question we can consider the distracting effect the one "whom Jesus loved" seemed to have on Peter.

Death is a weighty matter. Still, when Jesus brought up Peter's death, Peter turned his attention from Jesus to "the disciple whom Jesus loved". However, the key here is not the topic of death or Peter's attention shifting from Jesus, it is his timing. He focused on the one whom "Jesus loved" as soon as the topic became death. Would Peter's mind have associated Lazarus with this topic? Naturally.

This event was only "the third time that Jesus shewed himself to his disciples, after that he was risen from the dead" (Fourth gospel 21:14). Even so, Jesus was not the sole focus of Peter's attention. The author (known to us as "the disciple whom Jesus loved") proved to be a distraction for Peter, just as he later became a distraction to those who spread the rumor that he would not die.

Being a distraction would surely conflict with the author's objective (cf. Fourth gospel 20:31). We have already discussed how this potential conflict would have provided a motive for the author to remain anonymous. The question for you is: Do the facts support the conclusion that this was Lazarus, writing anonymously to avoid any hindrance to his goal?

The Humbleness Question

The idea that Lazarus would forgo using his name to avoid becoming a distraction to others would be in line with the author's expressed intent. After he was raised from the dead, Lazarus became an attraction for people (Fourth gospel 12:9). If he was also the God-inspired writer of the fourth gospel, then Lazarus would have been more than willing to avoid claiming authorship, rather than taking the risk of interfering with the reader's focus on Jesus.

"The disciple whom Jesus loved" may not be a very humble sounding term but we know it is an accurate description, since it was written under the inspiration of God – and note the timing here also. The author began referring to himself by this term only after he reported that "they came not for Jesus sake only, but that they might see Lazarus also".

It is common to hear people claim John was humble because of the author's anonymity. But this author was not John, so any attributes that one may want to infer about this author do not apply to John. If this author's effort to remain anonymous is an indication he was humble, then this quality pertains to the author whoever he was, including Lazarus.

Likewise, another fact may also imply humility on the part of Lazarus. This gospel tells of the raising of Lazarus and the subsequent public response, but notice that **the author didn't record a single word that was spoken by Lazarus**. We have no way to know if humility was the reason for either this or his anonymity. Still, it is worthwhile to note these things so that you can weigh all of the data regarding the author's character (i.e., Lazarus' character).

Names in Scripture

The belief that a man might forgo his name isn't foreign to the Bible. The disciples of Jesus were quite willing to change their names. Simon became Peter (Lu. 6:14), Saul became Paul (Acts 13:9), etc. Further, this practice was not new. Abram became Abraham way back in Genesis 17:5. In addition, the Bible often uses multiple names for people. James and John were surnamed, "Boanerges" (Mk. 3:17), Thomas was, "called Didymus" (Fourth gospel 21:2), and "Judas" (not Iscariot) was also called, "Thaddaeus" (cf. Lu. 6:16, Mk. 3:18).

Thus, it is at least compatible with scripture to suggest that Lazarus may have stopped using his name. Did he do this? If he was the unnamed author of the fourth gospel, then, in so far as this gospel is concerned, the answer is yes. As the jury you must decide, first, if scripture can prove that this author was not John. If so, then your next job is to decide if the biblical evidence indicates that this author was Lazarus. Hopefully you have been convinced, but we will look at one final piece of evidence that might help to persuade anyone who is still unsure.

The Other Murder Plot

Lazarus had an effect on "many of the Jews", for we're told that "by reason of him [Lazarus] many of the Jews went away, and believed on Jesus" (Fourth gospel 12:11). Of course, this may have been due solely to the fact that he had been raised from the dead. But it is also true that if Lazarus had been a known figure in the community, then that would have amplified the effect of the news of him being raised and several things hint at this idea. For example, after he died "many of the Jews" came to comfort his sisters (Fourth gospel 11:19), and even after four days "the Jews" were still seen "weeping" (Fourth gospel 11:33). In addition to his well attended memorial service, the body of Lazarus was in a cave tomb with a rock door (Fourth gospel 11:38), which sounds very much like the kind of tomb that we see associated with a rich man, Joseph of Arimathea (Mt. 27:57-60). Moreover, once when Lazarus and his sisters threw a supper for Jesus, his sister Mary anointed Jesus with "a pound" of "very costly" ointment (Fourth gospel 12:1-3). This, too, may be another indication that their household had no shortage of money.

Regardless, "the chief priests consulted that they might put Lazarus also to death; because that by reason of him many of the Jews went away, and believed on Jesus" (Fourth gospel 12:10-11). We can see that in the time between the raising of Lazarus and the plot to kill him, a ground swell of response to this miracle started to develop among the people (cf. Fourth gospel 12:18). Also, as word of the raising of Lazarus spread, the religious leaders would have had even more reason to want to dispose of him.

<u>Lazarus was the only one besides Jesus who was the object of a murder plot by the "chief priests"</u> prior to Pentecost. The "chief priests" did not plot to kill all of the disciples of Jesus, and they did not target just any random "friend" of Jesus. These men wanted to get rid of Lazarus specifically.

The thing to consider is that the "chief priests" knew that Lazarus had been raised from the dead – and they knew of the public's fascination with him and the impact that he was having on the people (Fourth gospel 11:46-47, 12:9-11 & 18). The "chief priests" may have known Lazarus as a figure in that community before Jesus raised him from the dead, but after he was raised they knew him as the man that they wanted to kill (Fourth gospel 12:10). These facts from the biblical record are relevant because they reveal that Lazarus was known unto the "chief priests".

Which Disciple Was Known?

Now, remember that the author twice tells us the "other disciple" was "known unto the high priest" (Fourth gospel 18:15 & 16). As shown earlier, this helps to prove John could not be the "other disciple, whom Jesus loved". The case for John faces a truly insurmountable problem here. On the other hand, if this "other disciple" was actually Lazarus, then this fact can be reconciled with the biblical evidence.

Here too, as with all of the other Bible facts that were weighed in this study, it can be shown that the scriptures harmonize completely with Lazarus being "the other disciple, whom Jesus loved".

"Add Thou Not unto His Words"

Earlier this study noted that the title *The Gospel of John* was not in the original text. Since this title was added later, and since the actual words of the God-inspired writers of scripture can show that the John idea is not true, then we have a compelling reason to avoid promoting the idea that the one whom "Jesus loved" was John. Therefore, in this study the book that was written by "the disciple whom Jesus loved" has not been referenced by the misleading title *John/Gospel of John*, for doing so serves to perpetuate a false idea. Instead the work of this anonymous gospel author was referenced as the fourth gospel, which is a simple, true, and easy-to-understand way to refer to his book in terms of its location in the New Testament.

Those who reject the unbiblical John tradition (and who refer to the gospel in a way that does not promote that erroneous tradition) will no doubt have to endure ridicule and scornful looks from those who will not accept the biblical evidence on this issue. Nevertheless, those who are careful to refer to the gospel of "the disciple whom Jesus loved" by a term that does not promote the John error are justifiably encouraged by the verse, "Prove all things; hold fast that which is good" (1 Th. 5:21), for they are holding fast to the truth revealed in scripture.

Inspired scripture is what we are to rely on – not the things that men may add to it. "Every word of God *is* pure: he *is* a shield unto them that put their trust in him. Add thou not unto his words, lest he reprove thee, and thou be found a liar" (Pr. 30:5-6).

Chapter 7

THE BIBLE VERSUS TRADITION & MORE BIBLE FACTS TO CONSIDER

The Jury Summation

This study presented two cases: the case as to why the Apostle John was not "the disciple whom Jesus loved", the author of the fourth gospel, and the case for why that author was most likely Lazarus – all with God's word being the only authority cited. Below is a summary to help you weigh the evidence so you can render a verdict. (All of the verses were quoted earlier, so they will not be noted here.)

The evidence shows beyond a reasonable doubt that John was not the "other disciple" because:

- *The gospel writers treated them like different people.* The first three gospels totally omit the one whom "Jesus loved", but they often refer to John by name – and yet all of those events where John was referenced by name in the first three gospels are missing from the book that the one whom "Jesus loved" wrote.

- *The one whom "Jesus loved" wrote his gospel without identifying himself by name, but there is no evidence John ever avoided using his own name.* In fact, John identified himself by name repeatedly in the Book of Revelation, and this difference in behavior argues against the idea that the same man wrote both books.

- *"The disciple whom Jesus loved" enjoyed a one-of-a-kind bond with Jesus.* This can't be said of John, and the three times that Jesus took John aside with Peter and James do not single John out as having that relationship.

- *On the night that Jesus was arrested, John and the "other disciple" behaved differently.* John let Jesus down by falling asleep three times. In contrast, the "other disciple" went into the palace of the high priest with Jesus, and we only see him leave at a time well into the next day, when Jesus reassigned him.

- *The idea that the one whom "Jesus loved" was John relies on the false assumption that this author was one of "the twelve".* Paintings of "the twelve" alone with Jesus at the supper promote this error. But the details in scripture show Jesus and "the twelve" were not alone at that event, like the fact they were guests in someone's home. Besides this, the phrase "other disciple" itself indicates he was <u>not</u> one of "the twelve" but, rather, that he was one of those additional loyal disciples who had also followed Jesus. (See Appendix for more proof he was not one of "the twelve".)

- *If "the disciple whom Jesus loved" joined Jesus and "the twelve" after the supper, then this person could not be John.* Yet this is just what is indicated by the author's own record of events at that Passover – which skips the Lord's Table and opens with the foot washing, after which Jesus sat down "again".

- *The "other disciple" was a known associate of Jesus, and he was known to the high priest.* But <u>John was not known to the high priest</u>. It was only after Pentecost that the high priest first became acquainted with John.

- *The author's anonymity argues against the John idea.* At the end of this author's gospel, he listed "the *sons* of Zebedee" at the same time that he listed two "other" disciples and called himself the one whom "Jesus loved". He grouped John in with the apostles but he referred to himself anonymously at that point.

A preponderance of the evidence indicates that Lazarus was the "other disciple" because:

- *They had the identical relationship with Jesus.* "Jesus loved" the one "whom Jesus loved" and "Jesus loved" Lazarus – and they were unique in this regard. They were the only men who associated with Jesus during his ministry that were also singled out in scripture as being "loved" by Jesus (the key relationship).

- *The other three gospel writers treat these two alike.* They do not tell us that Lazarus was a friend of Jesus, or that Lazarus had supper with Jesus, or even that Lazarus was raised from the dead! Likewise, they never mention "the other disciple, whom Jesus loved", and they totally ignore his unique role in the key events of the closing days of Jesus' life.

- *The anonymous author treats Lazarus and himself in a parallel manner in his gospel.* Lazarus suddenly appears late in the text and he is only referenced a few times. In a highly similar way, "the disciple whom Jesus loved" also suddenly appears late in the gospel and he too is only referenced a few times.

- *One seems to replace the other in the gospel.* The last mention of Lazarus occurs before the first mention of the one whom "Jesus loved". The author ceased all references to Lazarus in the text and it was only after he did so that the author began referring to himself as the one whom "Jesus loved".

- *The suddenly famous one disappears, and then the anonymous one suddenly appears.* Right after the public's desire to see Lazarus is recounted, a transition occurs: he vanishes from the text, and the term "Jesus loved" (that had only been used of him) then begins to be used by the author in anonymous references to himself – "the disciple whom Jesus loved", the "other disciple, whom Jesus loved", etc.

- *The experiences of Lazarus would produce the behavior exhibited by "the disciple whom Jesus loved".* Jesus gave a one-of-a-kind gift to Lazarus when he raised him from the dead. After that, Lazarus was different from the rest of Jesus' followers, and he would have been different from the man that he had been prior to that miracle. Jesus' relationship to the one whom "Jesus loved" and the behavior of this "other disciple" befit what one would expect if he was the raised-from-the-dead Lazarus.

- *The Bible reveals that both sat with Jesus.* The last time Lazarus is seen in the Bible he is sitting with Jesus at a table. Similarly, the first time the one whom "Jesus loved" is seen he is leaning on Jesus at a table.

- *When confronted with the "linen" evidence, the "other disciple" became the first one who "believed".* This reaction befits Lazarus – the one person in scripture who was most likely to be profoundly moved by the sight of the "linen clothes" and the "napkin", since he had been wearing similar wrappings for four days at the time he was raised from the dead.

- *The "not die" rumor about "the disciple whom Jesus loved" points to Lazarus.* Lazarus was raised from the dead. Jesus said, "whosoever liveth and believeth in me shall never die" just prior to raising him. Knowing either fact might cause a rush to judgment about Jesus' words, "If I will that he tarry till I come" and result in the rumor that was misconstrued from them (especially if it was known he "believed" first).

- *The "other disciple" was anonymous and Lazarus had a motive to become anonymous.* When the people came "not for Jesus' sake only" but to "see Lazarus also", surely Lazarus knew that the focus belonged on Jesus and not on him. Likewise, the author's intent was to lead people to Jesus, and he concealed his identity, thus he apparently felt that this was needed in order to achieve that objective.

- *When Peter's death was foretold he turned to "the disciple whom Jesus loved".* This could be because he associated "the disciple whom Jesus loved" with the issue of death, a topic that would undeniably be forever associated with Lazarus by all those who knew him.

- *The "other disciple" was a known associate of Jesus and was known to the high priest; both fit Lazarus.* He was a "friend" of Jesus and the apostles. Upon his death "many of the Jews" turned out, some still weeping four days later. When Lazarus was raised the "chief priests" sought to kill Jesus but thereafter many Jews "came not for Jesus sake only, but that they might see Lazarus also". So the "chief priests" conspired to kill him too because "by reason of him many of the Jews" believed on Jesus.

The First Disciples

The evidence presented thus far should have been sufficient to justify the goals put forth earlier. The Bible does have other items that are related to the facts we have considered. However, the verdict you have already reached is not likely to be altered by the three supplemental passages we will look at now. Still, these items are worth noting, for they can help to shed some added light on the unnamed "other disciple".

For example, consider what we are told about the first disciples of Jesus. The first chapter of the fourth gospel tells of a day when John the Baptist saw Jesus "coming unto him" and he went on to call Jesus, "the Lamb of God", to testify that the Spirit "abode upon him", and to "bare record that this is the Son of God" (Fourth gospel 1:29-34). The next day, Jesus returned and John the Baptist once again called him, "the Lamb of God", and then it says that two of the disciples of John the Baptist, "heard him speak, and they followed Jesus" (Fourth gospel 1:35-37).

We are told that these two disciples who went with Jesus, "abode with him that day" (Fourth gospel 1:38-39). These two were the very first individuals that the scripture says, "followed Jesus". Now, be careful to pay close attention to what the next two verses say, and more importantly, what they do not say.

"One of the two which heard John *speak,* and followed him, was Andrew, Simon Peter's brother. He first findeth his own brother Simon, and saith unto him, We have found the Messias, which is, being interpreted, the Christ" (Fourth gospel 1:40-41). In the subsequent verses, we see that Andrew brought his brother to meet Jesus, and that the following day Jesus found Philip (Fourth gospel 1:42-43).

Furthermore, we see that these original three (Andrew, Peter, and Philip) became loyal disciples and that they were eventually selected to be among "the twelve" (Mt. 10:2-3, Mk. 3:16-18, Lu. 6:14). But who have we forgotten here? Did you notice that there is one person who seems to vanish from the scene?

What happened to that other disciple of John the Baptist who was abiding with Jesus along with Andrew? As far as we can tell, Andrew and that second, unnamed individual were the first ones who "followed Jesus". Andrew's name is recorded here, and he gets mentioned in all of the gospels. Yet the other man that was one of those first two disciples is not named here, and we do not find him referenced at all outside of this passage. Did he just suddenly disappear? Was he of no importance? Or is there another possibility?

Another Possibility

The unnamed "disciple whom Jesus loved" is the only gospel author who tells of this unidentified ex-disciple of John the Baptist that followed Jesus. So, another possibility is that this unnamed follower of Jesus eventually became the unnamed author of the only book that mentions him. Perhaps one of the first two followers of Jesus amounted to nothing and merited no further mention. But it could also be that the unnamed gospel author decided to keep himself unnamed in his reporting on these first disciples.

Obviously, the bond between Jesus and the one whom "Jesus loved" didn't appear out of thin air. That relationship existed for some time prior to the Last Supper (where "the disciple whom Jesus loved" was first introduced). In light of this, is it conceivable that the unnamed "other disciple" was there from the beginning of Jesus' ministry? Yes. But can any other verses help to establish this? Yes. In Acts 1:21-22, Peter refers to men who, "companied with us all the time that the Lord Jesus went in and out among us, Beginning from the baptism of John, unto the same day that he [Jesus] was taken up". Although we cannot know for sure if Peter's words included the person who was present with Andrew that day, it is possible this unnamed early follower of Jesus was in that group. It is up to you to weigh this as you see fit. (Those who think the Apostle John wrote the fourth gospel will often claim this early follower *was* John. Yet, absolutely nothing in scripture justifies believing John met Jesus **before** Peter did. The opposite is actually true, for scripture indicates Jesus met Peter before he met both James and John.)

Clearly, there is not enough evidence to prove the anonymous author of this gospel was the same one who, along with Andrew, left John the Baptist to follow Jesus on that day. Nevertheless, this idea is worth considering, and would, of course, explain the origin of "the disciple whom Jesus loved" prior to Jesus' last Passover. Moreover, if this was Lazarus, then the episode helps to explain: (a) the origin of the relationship he had with Jesus, and (b) why he was called a "friend" of Jesus and the apostles.

Also, just prior to telling how Martha and Mary sent word of their ill brother to Jesus, the author had said Jesus, "went away again beyond Jordan into the place where John at first baptized; and there he abode" (Fourth gospel 10:40). So, their appeal came when Jesus was in the area. This, likewise, would place John the Baptist in the vicinity of Bethany at the time those two disciples left him to begin following Jesus. (The KJV calls this area, "Bethabara" (Fourth gospel 1:28), while others translate it, "Bethany". So the early link to Lazarus' home town is obscured in the KJV.)

Mark's Mystery Man

There may also be a unique link to Lazarus in Mark 14:43-53, which tells us about the night Jesus was betrayed and arrested. In Mark 14:50 we read, "And they all forsook him, and fled". You would think after the disciples fled there wouldn't be anyone left to stand with Jesus. However, immediately after this verse, we find an extremely curious reference that calls attention to the fact that at that point in time, one person still remained with Jesus – an unnamed "young man"!

Mark 14:51-52 tells us, "And there followed him [Jesus] a certain young man, having a linen cloth cast about *his* naked body; and the young men laid hold on him: And he left the linen cloth and fled from them naked". This is something that was not mentioned in the other gospels. Still, since it is part of inspired scripture, God must have wanted us to have this information. So, let's think carefully about the questions that are raised by these two verses.

One question is, why would this unnamed "young man" remain with Jesus after the rest of the disciples had fled? If he was Lazarus, then we know why he might have remained. Yet, this "young man" then fled too. So, how was his behavior different from that of the ones who "forsook" Jesus in Mark 14:50? It appears that he fled for a different reason.

Notice that Mark 14:51 takes the time to tell us the details of how this "young man" was clothed, having only a linen cloth covering his nakedness. Also, note that Mark 14:52 says he fled away naked. So what, you ask? When the others "forsook" Jesus "and fled", the implication is that they did so out of fear for their own safety. However, this "young man" left "naked", so this may suggest that he fled out of shame or embarrassment. We are told that they "laid hold on him" (Mk. 14:51b). The natural response to being grabbed is to pull away or to try to shake free, especially if one is grabbed without warning. So this is most likely how he came to be stripped, for the next words say, "And he left the linen cloth, and fled from them naked" (Mk. 14:52). No doubt startled to find himself being seized and suddenly naked, it was at that point that this "young man" then fled also.

This "young man" fled too, yet his actions are set apart from the rest of the disciples who forsook Jesus that night. Is it possible even the fear of death could not motivate Lazarus to flee, but unexpectedly being stripped naked might cause him to flee out of embarrassment in the heat of the moment?

Even after Lazarus was raised from the dead, he was still a human being, subject to the influence of emotions. After the mob left, he either retrieved the "linen cloth" or got something else to wear, and then proceeded to follow Jesus, as did Peter. Now, we will look to see if any evidence exists that might connect this "young man" to Lazarus.

A Fashion Statement?

In telling us this unnamed "young man" was the last follower of Jesus to flee from Gethsemane on that fateful night, scripture twice calls attention to this "young man's" attire. Twice we see references to the "linen cloth" this "young man" was wearing (Mk. 14:51 & 52), and both verses note this cloth was the only thing covering his otherwise "naked" body. So, why did God inspire this author to include these details? Perhaps he was led to record them because they can shed some additional light on this unnamed "young man".

Earlier in this study, the significance of "linen" clothes was discussed. Remember that our English word "linen" was used to translate several different Greek words, but that two of these always refer to the cloth covering a corpse, with the only exception being found here in Mark 14:51-52.

Why would this "young man" have chosen to wear a material that was used by the Jews to bury their dead? (Fourth gospel 19:40). Is it possible that this unnamed "young man" was indicating that he had already been dead or that he did not fear death? Or perhaps it was his way of indicating that he was a changed man, who reckoned himself dead to sin but alive unto God, the mindset that we see encouraged by Paul in Romans 6:11? Whatever the reason, this possible link between the unnamed "young man" and Lazarus (the unnamed "disciple whom Jesus loved") can be seen when one takes the time to examine the "linen" evidence that the Bible provides.

Enough Evidence?

An unnamed "young man" dressed in "linen" was the last one with Jesus when he was arrested, and every other time this Greek word for "linen" was used it was only in reference to Jesus' dead body (Mt. 27:59, Mk. 15:46(2x), Lu. 23:53). Is this enough evidence to suggest that this "young man" may have been Lazarus? Surely we cannot prove it for certain, yet, before you decide on this, consider one more fact.

Other than Jesus, this "young man" was the only person who the arresting mob sought to seize. They let the rest of the disciples go, but then they "laid hold on him" (Mk. 14:51). Why did they treat him differently from the disciples who were allowed to leave unhindered? There was only one man who the "chief priests" sought to kill at that point besides Jesus – they "consulted that they might put Lazarus also to death" (Fourth gospel 12:10). Even this, however, is not sufficient to prove that this was Lazarus.

Still, given the curious statements of Mark 14, which highlight the fact that this "young man" was the last person to leave Jesus at Gethsemane, this potential link to Lazarus is worth thinking about.

Once again, as you consider these additional items, please remember that the evidence that was previously presented herein regarding both Lazarus and John is intended to stand on its own. These supplemental items are being discussed simply as a way of tying up a few loose ends.

More than a Story?

Now we'll look at some of the unique parallels between a story that is told in the Gospel of Luke, and the facts that are reported by the anonymous author in his gospel (Fourth gospel 11:1-12:10, Lu. 16:19-31). As we do, keep one thing in mind: although Jesus did use stories to teach, scripture also indicates that Jesus was a prophet (Mk. 6:4, Acts 3:22-26).

In the story taught by Jesus in Luke 16, he referred to two characters, a "rich man" and a man named "Lazarus", both of whom died (Lu. 16:19, 20 & 22). The "rich man" then found himself "being in torments" (Lu. 16:23), and he proceeded to make some requests. To start with, he sought relief and, oddly enough, in his appeal he included the petition, "send Lazarus..." (Lu. 16:24). The "rich man" was then told why that could not happen (Lu. 16:25-26). Following this, the "rich man" made another appeal involving "Lazarus", "send him [Lazarus] to my father's house: for I have five brethren; that he [Lazarus] may testify unto them" (Lu. 16:27-28).

Notice what Jesus did here with this story. The dead "rich man" was asking if someone named "Lazarus" could return from the dead to "testify" unto his "brethren", who were still alive.

Jesus also underscores the fact this was precisely what the "rich man" was requesting. When the "rich man" was told that his brethren "have Moses and the prophets" (Lu. 16:29) he protested, because he thought sending Lazarus back from the dead would lead them to respond differently – "if one went unto them from the dead, they will repent" (Lu. 16:30).

Sadly, however, the "rich man" was informed, "If they hear not Moses and the prophets, neither will they be persuaded, though one rose from the dead" (Lu. 16:31). Jesus ended the story here.

Now, try to imagine the effect this teaching would have had on those who actually heard Jesus give this message, especially his disciples. The day the disciples heard Jesus speak these words it is likely they assumed that this story was no different than Jesus' other teaching stories. But what do you suppose went through their minds when they later saw part of this story come true? That is, when an individual named Lazarus did rise from the dead!

Who Was Jesus Speaking About?

Some will try to take the 'moral of the story' and apply it to the situation of the high priest, rulers, elders, and scribes who refused to repent after the resurrection of Jesus. While this might appear to be a good fit, let's take a closer look at this.

To begin with, note the contrast between the way Jesus ended the story ("if they hear not Moses and the prophets, neither will they be persuaded though one rose from the dead") and the response to the news of the resurrection of Jesus, which **has** been persuading people for the last 2000 years!

Moreover, consider this fact. In the scriptures the resurrected Jesus did not appear to unbelievers. After the resurrection, every recorded appearance of Jesus was to those who believed or would believe. He did not appear before the chief priests, elders, and/or their council to "testify" unto them.

These facts seem to hinder a comparison between the resurrected Jesus and the person who was requested by the "rich man" in Luke 16:30, the one who the "rich man" was sure would bring about repentance in those who already had "Moses and the prophets" (Lu. 16:29).

While it has frequently been related to Jesus' resurrection, his witnesses in the New Testament, and the good news of the gospel, this story might be better understood if we consider the possibility that in Luke 16:19-31, Jesus was articulating a prophecy. (Jesus' delay and words prior to raising Lazarus may well support this idea (cf. Fourth gospel 11:4, 6-7 & 14-15).)

The Luke 16 story has several parallels to the real life Lazarus. In both cases Lazarus died, but in the story we don't see him raised, we only hear the request. Also, while there are no words of Lazarus recorded in the Bible, it is certain that he did "testify" about Jesus to those with whom he spoke.

In addition, Lazarus became a living testimony to the power of Jesus and because of him "many of the Jews went away and believed on Jesus". But just like the response described in Luke 16, the Jewish leaders (who had "Moses and the prophets") were not persuaded – even though a Lazarus *was* sent to them from the dead. Eyewitnesses to this miracle "went their ways to the Pharisees, and told them what things Jesus had done". Yet, instead of repenting, "the chief priests and Pharisees" plotted to kill Jesus (Fourth gospel 11:46-53). The "chief priests" sought to kill Lazarus also (Fourth gospel 12:10). So, was the reaction described by Jesus in Luke 16:31 a prophecy of this response? As with the two other supplemental passages, it's up to you to ponder this food for thought. Now, however, we will return to the main thrust of this study to provide a wrap-up and to tackle some questions that are likely to remain.

In Conclusion

Most of us bought the idea that John was the author of the gospel that bears his name because:
- This is what we have been told
- It has been called this for a long time
- This is what 'all' the scholars seem to say
- The gospel we read has this 'title' added to it
- Etc.

These might seem like separate arguments, but, in fact, the same mistaken assumption underlies them all. They all rely on a non-Bible source, i.e., trusting someone else's judgment. These 'reasons' don't require us to search the scriptures; rather, they rely on someone else to have already done this job.

But, what if others now and in the past have done the same? Who is left to search the scriptures? The scholars? Isn't it normal for them to rely on the work of scholars who preceded them (like judges rely on prior rulings)? What happens if successive generations tended to rely on the work of those who have preceded them? Furthermore, what happens if an error gets introduced into this sequence early on? If an error went unchallenged long enough it might eventually become accepted as truth and correcting this error would grow more difficult as time went on – because its 'historical acceptance' would become a rationale for assuming that this idea must be true.

Clearing up a long accepted misconception is a big challenge, but the Bible is up to it. What should come out of this is that we receive the correction scripture offers so we can benefit from the blessings that follow when we let the Bible speak for itself. There was never any **biblical** support for the John idea, as you now know. <u>The fact this error has fooled so many so long should be a wake-up call to us all</u>. Let this inspire you to search the scriptures more diligently in the future. Instead of thinking you can just adopt the opinions of others on biblical matters, or that some 'expert's' judgment must necessarily be better than your own, make use of the judgment God gave to you and be open to the truth presented by God's word.

This study presented reasoning that relies on the Bible only. On the other hand, those who seek to defend the John idea are forced to use arguments that ultimately rest on *everything but the Bible*. Yet this is not clear until we begin focusing on this issue.

The efforts to defend the John idea actually reveal there is no biblical justification for teaching it. Take a look. Those who promote the John tradition do not quote scripture to justify their belief, rather, they defend it by citing this-or-that non-Bible source (i.e., an 'early church' personality, majority opinion, historical tradition, etc.). But if the Bible justified their teaching of this tradition, they would quote scripture and allow it to prove the point, instead of relying on hearsay and the opinions of men to make their case. No amount of non-Bible consensus is ever sufficient to overcome the truth that is revealed by scripture. **The primary source is always the best evidence** – and on biblical matters that source is God's word.

If we look to somebody else to read the Bible and search the scriptures for us, then we will adopt their mistakes and any errors they pass along to us. Scripture shows educated religious men sometimes believe ideas and promote traditions contrary to the word of God (Mk. 7:13, Col. 2:8, et al.). So, belief by men is clearly not a reliable indicator of whether or not an idea is true. Yet confidence in tradition is precisely what leads many to fall for circular reasoning: e.g., 'We know John wrote it, because it's his gospel', or 'It's called the Gospel of John, because John wrote it' (even though the author said nothing of the kind). Others fall prey to error in assuming 'John must have written the Gospel of John, because this is what everyone else thinks'. This still relies on others to have the truth but it also falsely presumes a large number of people cannot be wrong concurrently. However, even if 'everybody' seems to think an idea is true, the fact is agreement with God's word is the biblical test of truth, not agreement among men.

Why have the vast majority of scholars and books misidentified the author of the fourth gospel? How could the truth have been missed by so many for so long? Besides the reasons discussed above, there is another possibility that we should consider. It may be that God is opening the eyes of people to this truth in order to humble us and draw us into a deeper reliance on His word. At the very least, the exposing of the John error should prove man has not already discovered all of the Bible's truths.

Where Do We Go from Here?

Some will just ignore this issue and the Bible facts related to it. Still, they and any who promote the John tradition will continue to face one daunting question: <u>If what they teach is biblical, why doesn't a single verse justify teaching this idea</u>? Also, if the Bible can prove John was not the "other disciple", does that truth not matter? In any case, some will be persuaded by the biblical evidence presented herein and these final thoughts are directed to that group.

If we discover evidence that indicates we might be mistaken on a matter, what should we do? The scriptures can prove the Apostle John was not the author of the fourth gospel, but men who relied on non-Bible sources ended up attributing it to him. You have also seen there is a substantial amount of biblical evidence which supports the conclusion the unnamed "disciple whom Jesus loved" was Lazarus of Bethany. What is unique about this insight is it can be seen after almost 2,000 years and, like a watermark of truth, it provides a powerful argument for the reliability of the Bible we have today.

The Apostle Paul wrote, "All scripture *is* given by inspiration of God, and *is* profitable for doctrine, for reproof, for correction, for instruction in righteousness..." (2Tim. 3:16), and this is still true today. We also are told, "Blessed *is* that man that maketh the LORD his trust, and respecteth not the proud, nor such as turn aside to lies" (Ps. 40:4). Knowing the true identity of the one whom "Jesus loved" is surely not necessary to have eternal life. But **respect for God's word is required** – for one cannot believe Jesus died and rose "according to the scriptures" (1Cor. 15:3-4) apart from the foundation of God's word! This is why we dare not intentionally ignore truth on topics we deem are not 'critical'. We do not get to 'agree-to-disagree' with truth, since truth is not a matter of opinion. Specifically, the truth on this issue is important because it illustrates how the Bible can correct us and it encourages us to seek the truth, "not in the words which man's wisdom teacheth, but which the Holy Ghost teacheth; comparing spiritual things with spiritual" (cf. 1Cor. 2:13).

Respect for the Authority of God's Word

Of "the LORD" who said, "them that honour me I will honour" (1Sa. 2:30), we are also told, "...thou hast magnified thy word above all thy name" (Ps. 138:2). So, honoring God's word will surely yield future benefits. Nevertheless, just like those in Mark 7:13 who made the word of God of no effect by their tradition, some will cling to the John idea even though it is unbiblical and, in order to justify doing so, they will go on citing non-Bible sources that agree with them. This serves as an excuse for adding John's name to the text, but it ultimately undermines the authority of God's word.

If discovering that the Bible can disprove the John tradition cannot motivate people to reconsider how they determine whether or not an idea is true, then they'll reap the consequences of that decision. To avoid having to respond to Bible evidence that might prove them wrong, some rush to brush aside the issue by asking, 'What difference does it make?' as a rhetorical question – and this sets a dangerous precedent. The danger lies in acting as if we get to decide when it's okay to ignore the truth. Those who want to stick with the John idea need an excuse to avoid scripture/change the subject, so they will imply that 'It doesn't matter.' However, while the truth may not matter to them, their decision to ignore it matters a lot. If a wrong idea is believed/taught in ignorance, that's one thing, but what about after one is exposed to the truth? Is it right for one to promote any idea as if it were biblical when they <u>know</u> they cannot cite a single verse that would justify teaching that idea?

As was shown herein, testing our beliefs by the standard of God's word can help to expose and correct misconceptions we might have. So, one difference should be that you will find yourself being less likely to simply assume a teaching is true, and more inclined to subject ideas to biblical scrutiny, in order to see if they are true or not. A biblically based inquiry is not a threat to the truth, but the unguarded intake of information can be hazardous. We cannot afford to be hasty in learning or uncritical about the things that we read/hear. (Read Mark 4:14-25 to see what led Jesus to warn, "Take heed what ye hear"!) In Acts 17:11 and other passages, <u>the Bible indicates that it is an honorable practice for us to use scripture to verify the truth of any idea, belief, or tradition.</u>

Regardless, traditions like the John idea are often treasured more than truth, so discussion of the Bible evidence will no doubt be discouraged by those who merely pay lip service to the Bible's authority. Moreover, this idea has been accepted for so long that many will refuse even to consider the possibility it could be wrong. Others will scoff and act as if any challenge to the John tradition is impossible or inconsequential. You know that it is **not** impossible for this type of error to be made, but is it really true teaching some error is okay? Or might the decision to intentionally ignoring scripture in order to carry on an unbiblical tradition lead to other problems?

Scripture contains warnings against adding to God's word and yet, to some degree, this happens each time John's name is added to the reading of a passage about the one "whom Jesus loved". While it is easy to slip and add our ideas to the plain reading of God's word when we are discussing or studying Bible matters, those who love the truth must guard against this tendency. This point is not meant as a condemnation of those who are communicators of God's word. Surely teachers have a responsibility to be as biblically accurate as they can possibly be, but they can make mistakes just like the rest of us. None of us will always be right, so the wise move is always to **invite** <u>biblical correction</u> and to receive the truth thankfully when God's word offers it to us.

When a question of biblical accuracy is being raised, which do you think is the more appropriate response: (a) 'What difference does it make?', or (b) 'show me in scripture'? Those who love the truth will welcome correction, while others will find an excuse to change the subject to avoid the light of scripture. By asserting that it makes no difference, they act as if there is no need to pay attention to what scripture says on the topic. Sadly, many will elect to turn a blind eye to facts in the Bible that threaten to challenge one of their preferred beliefs. Conversely, the 'show me' response invites biblical correction.

What is at stake in this matter? The answer is respect for the authority of God's word. For when God's word says one thing, but a person who claims to believe in God's word says something else, then clearly scripture is not their authority on that issue. The real test on any issue is whether or not we will receive the correction that is offered by scripture and the benefit of receiving that correction (just as in the matter of "the disciple whom Jesus loved") is its ability to inspire a greater reliance upon God's word.

Hebrews 11:6 tells us that God "is a rewarder of them that diligently seek him", and that condition "diligently" indicates that mere Bible knowledge isn't the goal. What you have studied herein is not some curious item of Bible trivia. It is a serious Bible issue that confirms the reliability of scripture and the need to "prove all things". Although it's been overlooked by so many for so long, the beauty of this insight is that **the Bible has always pointed to the truth!** Still, let us remember that even the disciples did not realize some things about the scriptures until Jesus opened their eyes to those things, as we see in Luke 24:45, "Then opened he [Jesus] their understanding, that they might understand the scriptures". Might God act similarly today, by opening our understanding to things we had previously overlooked?

Even today, God can still reveal truth through the Bible, as this study has shown. Yet the truth also causes division, just like Jesus said he would bring (Lu. 12:51), for some will unite behind the truth while others will oppose it – falling on one side or the other in response to the sword of God's word, which is "a discerner of the thoughts and intents of the heart" (He. 4:12). Love rejoices in the truth (cf. 1Cor. 13:6). So if it turns out something we thought was true is actually unscriptural, then shouldn't we turn away from error, get back to God's word, and speak the truth in love? While much is said about why Jesus was born or the reason he came into the world, here too, the Bible is better than hearsay and it would be wise to align our thinking with scripture on this point also (see pg. 146).

If your eyes have been opened to a truth that others have missed, then the question you must ask is: <u>If so many could be wrong about this, what else could they be wrong about?</u> The answer is, anything not taught in scripture! And if you missed this truth, then this may indicate that something was lacking in your own Bible study method. So take seriously the admonition to, "prove all things" (1Th. 5:21), and heed Psalm 118:8. "A little leaven leaveneth the whole lump" (Gal 5:9). This is why deviating from God's word is not a 'minor issue'; rather, it is a perilous habit that opens one up to deception. Read the Bible with care to make sure it truly says what you think it says and when you find an issue where scripture proves you were wrong, then thank God for the correction and boldly stand with the truth. Praise be to God.

"To every *thing there is* a season, and a time to every purpose under the heaven" (Ecc. 3:1).

Appendix

The "Other Disciple" Believed First

"Then went in also that other disciple, which came first to the sepulchre, and he saw, and believed" (Fourth gospel 20:8). Earlier editions of this book did note that the "other disciple" was the first one in scripture who "believed" after Jesus' resurrection, but it was in the context of discussing why he reacted this way. This led to a key piece of evidence being overlooked – the significance of **when** he "believed".

This is the record of what happened to Peter and the "other disciple" on resurrection morning: "The first *day* of the week cometh Mary Magdalene early, when it was yet dark, unto the sepulchre, and seeth the stone taken away from the sepulchre. Then she runneth, and cometh to Simon Peter, and to the other disciple, whom Jesus loved, and saith unto them, They have taken away the Lord out of the sepulchre, and we know not where they have laid him. Peter therefore went forth, and that other disciple, and came to the sepulchre. So they ran both together: and the other disciple did outrun Peter, and came first to the sepulchre. And he stooping down, *and looking in*, saw the linen clothes lying; yet went he not in. Then cometh Simon Peter following him, and went into the sepulchre, and seeth the linen clothes lie, And the napkin, that was about his head, not lying with the linen clothes, but wrapped together in a place by itself. Then went in also that other disciple, which came first to the sepulchre, and he saw, and believed. For as yet they knew not the scripture, that he must rise again from the dead. Then the disciples went away again unto their own home" (Fourth gospel 20:1-10).

The fourth gospel is the only book that tells of this "other disciple", so this is the only record of his reaction on that morning. At any rate, scripture says, "the other disciple did outrun Peter, and came first to the sepulcher" and that "he saw, and believed". (The author then emphasized, "as yet they knew not the scripture, that he must rise again from the dead" (Fourth gospel 20:9). Therefore, he made it clear that he "believed" even though neither he nor Peter had yet realized that scripture had foretold the resurrection.) This is the first time after the resurrection the Bible refers to anyone believing, so we can see that he "believed" before the rest of the disciples.

More importantly, this information proves the "other disciple" was not one of "the twelve" apostles because of the timing of their belief. He "believed" early on the morning of the resurrection, but they did not believe until later that day, after they saw Jesus. This point of contrast with the apostles can be seen in verses like this, "Afterward he [Jesus] appeared unto the eleven as they sat at meat, and upbraided them with their unbelief and hardness of heart, because they believed not them which had seen him after he was risen" (Mk. 16:14).

Despite hearing from those who had seen the risen Jesus, the "unbelief" of "the eleven" persisted until late on resurrection day. They couldn't even be convinced by the two who had been taught by Jesus earlier that day on the road to Emmaus (when "he expounded unto them in all the scriptures the things concerning himself" (Lu. 24:13-27)). These two had told these things to "the eleven" (Lu. 24:33-34) but, still, the apostle's "unbelief" continued until they personally saw the resurrected Jesus.

The evidence presented in this study proved **whoever** the "other disciple" was, he was not John. Now we have proof he was not any of "the twelve". That disciple "believed" <u>before he saw Jesus</u>, while "the eleven" were in "unbelief" <u>until they saw Jesus</u>. He "believed" early on resurrection morning and that sets the author of the fourth gospel in stark contrast to the "unbelief" of "the eleven" later that same day.

The Bible Versus Non-Bible Sources

Those who stick with the John idea in spite of the biblical evidence to the contrary will surely go on citing non-Bible sources as if that justifies promoting the John tradition. But now they will have to ignore, or explain away, yet one more contrast between the "other disciple" and "the twelve". Either way, it's never wise to dismiss what the Bible says. When people quote non-Bible sources to defend an idea because they cannot cite scripture that would justify teaching that idea, then that in itself should tell us something. It should be a big red flag!

If we let our beliefs/the beliefs of others serve as the standard by which truth is judged, then what is our authority? The scholars of Jesus' day cited themselves as the measure of truth when they said, "Have any of the rulers or of the Pharisees believed on him?" (Fourth gospel 7:48). Here they are pointing to non-Bible sources (the beliefs of leaders) rather than quoting scripture to make their case. The same thing occurs when non-Bible sources are used to sell people on accepting the John idea. What no one has ever done is cite a single verse that actually justifies teaching that the one whom "Jesus loved" was John – not those who originated this unbiblical idea and not those who repeat their error unto this day.

This issue ultimately comes down to the Bible vs. tradition (i.e., non-Bible sources). Those who will ignore the testimony of scripture on this issue give themselves artistic license to trust non-Bible sources over scripture whenever they choose to do so.

A Better Bible Study Method

Instead of relying on men who cite other men *who cite other men*, ask yourself: Why don't they just cite scripture if **it** truly teaches what they say it does? As this study has shown, <u>relying on the word of God to be the standard for determining what is biblical is a better Bible study method</u>. (What method do **you** use to determine whether something is true or not?)

We must be careful to resist appeals to man's wisdom or we risk being lured into believing things simply because others believe them. Teachers will often cite 'the commonly accepted interpretation' or 'consensus' to sell an idea. The problem is that such appeals falsely imply that agreement among men is a reliable measure of truth, even though one doesn't have to look far in scripture to disprove this notion.

Don't get stampeded into following the crowd. We ought to fear God rather than men, and it makes sense that this should apply to our Bible study also. Consider the source! If an idea is taught in scripture, then it's biblical. But if it's not taught in scripture, then we should not pretend that it is. The LORD said, "he that hath my word, let him speak my word faithfully" (Jer. 23:28b). So, ideas from non-Bible sources should not be substituted for, or added to, the word of God.

Moreover, we do not get to pick-and-choose when truth is important and when it doesn't matter. To do so is to act as if turning a blind eye to the facts in scripture is justified by declaring that truth matters only when we, or those we are following, say it does. Yet, if we grant ourselves or others the right to say when a truth in scripture can be ignored, then we've decided that a non-Bible source is to be esteemed more highly than the word of God itself, despite the biblical warnings against doing so. We will either fall into the trap of repeating the ideas of men, or we'll get in the habit of proving all things with scripture.

God's inspired writers repeatedly used terms like "as it is written" in upholding scripture as the standard of truth. The word of God is always reliable. So when we face an issue where God's word and the words of men are in conflict, we would be wise to consider the advice of Psalm 118:8, "*It is* better to trust in the LORD than to put confidence in man".

"The LORD Trieth the Hearts"

Was the John idea "from heaven, or of men"? This question is answered by the biblical evidence presented herein, for if a belief contradicts scripture then that idea is not "from heaven". Now, once we have seen that the John idea contradicts scripture, what should we say to those who point us back to non-Bible sources or urge us not to share this truth with others? At that point it may be best to respond as Peter and John did when they were told not to tell others the truth about Jesus, "Whether it be right in the sight of God to hearken unto you more than unto God, judge ye. For we cannot but speak the things which we have seen and heard" (Acts 4:19b-20).

In scripture, a test is often used to prove what is in one's heart (Ex. 16:4, Du. 8:16, Ps. 26:2, et al.), and the choice between tradition and truth that confronts us on this issue is, no doubt, also a test. God's will is for all men "to come unto the knowledge of the truth" (1Ti. 2:4). However, the Bible tells of many who would not do so, like those who "turn away *their* ears from the truth" (2Ti. 4:4), or those in leadership who actually "believed on" Jesus but would not acknowledge that truth because "they loved the praise of men more than the praise of God" (Fourth gospel 12:42-43). Did their response <u>matter</u>? If God's word challenges us on an issue, <u>does it make a difference</u> how we respond? One thing is certain, the children of God listen when God's word speaks: Jesus said, "He that is of God heareth God's words" (Fourth gospel 8:47). As it is written in Proverbs 17:3, "the LORD trieth the hearts".

To top off this study weigh the Postscript, the Addendum, and revisit the verses on page 4. For more Bible-only studies see TruthHunt.com

Get answers to additional questions on this topic, free Bible software and study tools, audio teaching, eBook versions and printer-friendly copies of this book, and more at TheDiscipleWhomJesusLoved.com

POSTSCRIPT

Jesus said "To this end was I born, and for this cause came I into the world, that I should bear witness unto the truth" (Fourth gospel 18:37).

"The LORD *is* nigh unto all them that call upon him, to all that call upon him in truth" (Ps. 145:18).

"Trust in the LORD with all thine heart; and lean not unto thine own understanding" (Pr. 3:5).

"Cease, my son, to hear the instruction *that causeth* to err from the words of knowledge" (Pr. 19:27).

"The fear of man bringeth a snare: but whoso putteth his trust in the LORD shall be safe" (Pr. 29:25).

"The fear of the LORD *is* the beginning of knowledge: *but* fools despise wisdom and instruction" (Pr. 1:7).

"He that refuseth instruction despiseth his own soul: but he that heareth reproof getteth understanding" (Pr. 15:32).

"Hear instruction, and be wise, and refuse it not" (Pr. 8:33).

"... reproofs of instruction *are* the way of life" (Pr. 6:23b).

"All scripture *is* given by inspiration of God, and *is* profitable for doctrine, for reproof, for correction, for instruction in righteousness" (2Ti. 3:16).

"He that is of God heareth God's words..." (Fourth gospel 8:47a).

"... the word of our God shall stand for ever" (Is. 40:8b).

"... thou hast magnified thy word above all thy name" (Ps. 138:2b).

"... thy word is truth" (Fourth gospel 17:17b).

"God *is* a Spirit: and they that worship him must worship *him* in spirit and in truth" (Fourth gospel 4:24).

"Finally, brethren, whatsoever things are true... think on these things" (Php. 4:8).

Addendum

This was added to encourage readers of this study to resist the efforts of those who try to bully them into keeping quiet about parts of scripture that argue against the traditions of men.

"Whatsoever Doth Make Manifest Is Light"

The Bible says, "whatsoever doth make manifest is light" (Eph. 5:13b). Therefore, by the principle of this verse, it is a good thing if the biblical evidence presented herein helps to make the truth manifest. So, why would anyone try to turn Bible students away from the light of scripture? Truly, only those who give a fair hearing to the evidence are in a position to say if truth was made manifest by this exercise in searching the scriptures. Still, some act as if glancing through this study, peeking at the back, or even refusing to hear a word of the evidence qualifies them to render a verdict on it. Yet we are told, "He that answereth a matter before he heareth *it*, it *is* folly and shame unto him" (Pr. 8:13). No jury would be allowed to offer a verdict if they refused to hear the evidence and only showed up for the jury summation. Likewise, true critical thinking on any biblical issue is not possible without first hearing the testimony of God's word on the matter.

Sadly, readers who share the truth on this issue will find the truth is not always welcome. But if one is offered evidence that can "make manifest" a truth on a topic and their response is equivalent to saying 'Turn off that light!', then where is the love of the truth? Dodging the issue, defensive anger, mocking, lukewarm indifference, etc. are clearly not responses that exhibit a love of the truth. So, what should be the response when biblical correction is being shared between members of the body of Christ? How about this for starters, "Teach me thy way, O LORD; I will walk in thy truth" (Ps. 86:11a)?

When urging believers to "walk as children of light" (Eph. 5:8) Paul's advice included this step, "Proving what is acceptable unto the Lord" (Eph. 5:10) and testing our beliefs by the word of God is one way to put this into practice. Moreover, a few verses earlier he offered this warning, "Let no man deceive you with vain words" (Eph. 5:6a) and this offers good counsel to every student of God's word – especially given the Bible's strong words of caution like this, "Add thou not unto his words, lest he reprove thee, and thou be found a liar" (Pr. 30:5-6).

Surely "vain words" would include words that appear to be in line with scripture which, in fact, are not justified by scripture (or worse yet, are actually in contradiction to God's word). A way to avoid being deceived by the error that naturally comes with such "vain words" is to get into the "prove all things" habit – testing the things we hear and read, along with the ideas we picked up in the past, by subjecting them to biblical scrutiny whenever we can.

"Judge Righteous Judgment"

"Judge not according to the appearance, but judge righteous judgment" (Fourth gospel 7:24). If we incorporate the principle of this verse into our Bible study method we will be much less likely to become ensnared by superficial arguments. Often "vain words" will appear reasonable at first glance, however, the light of God's word can reveal they do not line up with the truth. Therefore, we have to be diligent to judge the words of men by the word of God or we may end up doing exactly the opposite.

As this study has shown, it can seem wise to follow the crowd with their age old hand-me-down teaching but the air of truth which comes with the claim of 'consensus' is a deceptive lure. Even intellectual elites can be wrong, so one cannot just repeat what a teacher or scholar says. We need to be critical thinkers regarding everything we believe and are taught. Who has the power and authority to set God's word aside? Does a high IQ or a PhD give one that right? How about achieving a prominent church position or living in the second century? If a lot, or even a majority of people believe what someone says, does the authority of scripture become secondary at that point?

If our authority is God's word, then no matter who is teaching or what the issue is, we need to judge the truth by that standard. Psalm 138:2, in talking about the LORD, says, "thou hast magnified thy word above all thy name". Many other verses also make it clear the word of God ought to be held in the highest esteem. The will of God is, therefore, for his children to respect what scripture says.

Still, some will find an excuse to ignore God's will or even argue there is some virtue in suppressing the truth, so they can justify their loyalty to an unbiblical tradition. People who want to go on promoting the John idea even after they learn of biblical evidence to the contrary will act as if the words 'it doesn't matter' are a proper response on this issue. By hiding behind excuses like 'it is not a salvation issue', 'what really matters is the gospel', etc. they can make it sound like they are showing respect for God's word even as they are trampling on its authority and offer of correction. Truly, those who say such things reveal something about themselves; they show they do not know how to properly weigh an issue, for such words express just the opposite of respect for the word of God (by suggesting some issue is more important than the authority of God's word itself).

"Whether *Is* Greater"

"*Ye* fools and blind: for whether *is* greater, the gift, or the altar that sanctifieth the gift?" (Mt. 23:19). This rebuke was spoken to members of the religious elite who were misleading the people. Jesus here proved their opinion of what was important was not justified by scripture or logic, but actually ran counter to both. When they usurped the authority to declare what was important based on the sayings of men and not the word of God, the result was their false teachings debased the authority of God's word and turned people away from the truth.

As was noted earlier, it can be tempting to follow the words of men who appear to be wise. But Jesus reserved many harsh sayings for scholars and religious leaders. So, one should not think it is safe to adopt the teachings of men who hold positions of honor. If we drop our guard because we respect the person who is teaching, then we will be susceptible to any errors they present. Paul wrote, "we dare not make ourselves of the number, or compare ourselves with some that commend themselves: but they measuring themselves by themselves, and comparing themselves among themselves, are not wise" (2Cor. 10:12). So, obviously, following those who engage in the practice of "measuring themselves by themselves, and comparing themselves among themselves" is not a wise thing to do. Yet is that not a perfect description of those who think a 'consensus' among scholars or any other group is a good measure of truth? If it is, then you should be wary when someone cites a 'consensus' on an issue as if that was an appropriate or reliable measure of truth.

In posing this question, "How can ye believe, which receive honour one of another, and seek not the honour that *cometh* from God only?" (Fourth gospel 5:44), Jesus was clearly implying, "the honour that *cometh* from God only" is better. He also said, "He that is faithful in that which is least is faithful also in much: and he that is unjust in the least is unjust also in much" (Lu. 16:10). Moreover, we read, "A little leaven leaveneth the whole lump" (Gal 5:9). So, if one cannot honor God by **intentionally** misrepresenting the word of God, then this would be true on every issue. Therefore, one is wrong to think saying 'it doesn't matter', 'that is a secondary issue' or any such excuse can justify the act of shutting one's eyes and intentionally ignoring the authority of God's word on <u>any</u> issue.

The "unjust in the least" principal lets us know those who turn a blind eye to Bible facts on one issue will be willing to do likewise on other issues. Conversely, those who are faithful to God's word and change their belief to align with the facts in scripture in "that which is least" will also be faithful when it comes to more important matters. The ability to come up with high-sounding excuses for refusing biblical correction is not the mark of one who is seeking the honor that comes "from God only".

Read Matthew 23:13-24. Jesus' repudiation of the religious leaders who taught a false assessment of what is greater comes as part of an overall rebuke of their teachings and methods. Rather than pointing people to God's word and teaching them to rely on it as the standard of truth, they simply taught others to believe as they believed. Jesus proved them wrong by pointing out it is self-refuting to think the gift is more important than the altar, since the altar is what made the gift noteworthy. Likewise, to imply salvation or any other issue could be more important than God's word is just as self-refuting as thinking the gift matters more than the altar, for scripture is what establishes the truth regarding salvation or any other issue. "All scripture is given by inspiration of God" (2Ti. 3:16) and this is why the authority of scripture cannot be overcome by any non-Bible source – no matter what the issue is. It is also why those who seek the honor that comes "from God only" will respect the biblical evidence that proves the one "whom Jesus loved" was not John.

"The Fear of the LORD"

"The fear of the LORD is the beginning of knowledge: but fools despise wisdom and instruction" (Pr. 1:7). At the very least this fear would move one to be as accurate as possible when representing scripture, for the LORD said, "he that hath my word, let him speak my word faithfully" (Jer. 23:28b). Being faithful to an unbiblical tradition rather than to God's word is, therefore, certainly not God's will.

Is refusing biblical correction or suppressing the truth motivated by a fear of the LORD? No it is not. Those who act as if loyalty to their prior beliefs is a virtue that trumps respect for the authority of God's word are not doing so out of a fear of the LORD, even if they say they only do so when 'it doesn't really matter'.

Many benefits are said to follow the fear of the LORD and a willingness to hear God's word, be faithful to it, and humbly accept the rebuke and correction that it offers. The benefit of having scripture tear down a false tradition is <u>not</u> first and foremost that we can discover the truth on a particular issue. Rather, it is waking-up to the fact that something is wrong with our method of assessing truth on biblical issues. Learning we were wrong on any issue is not a bad thing, it is opportunity knocking. Not only the opportunity to grow in knowledge on that particular issue but, more importantly, if we can figure out what led us to be deceived on that issue, then we can work to improve our method of determining the truth on biblical issues.

As this study has shown, non-Bible sources can make an untrue idea appear to be 'pre-approved' truth. When we realize it is not safe to assume an idea is true merely because others have believed that idea, we will be less susceptible when non-Bible sources are used to sell an idea, or to discourage us from subjecting an idea to biblical scrutiny (by getting us to trust in a substitute for the authority of God's word and turning us away from searching the scriptures).

This book used two cases on the beloved disciple to show a need for a better Bible study method. Lord willing, the next book in this series will present case studies on a variety of topics to show how wrong methods cause our thinking about God's word to be conformed to this world, and this leads to many errors. Here again the aim will not primarily be to refute errors. Rather, it will be to identify the underlying causes of the errors and make the case for the need to transform our approach to scripture so it better reflects the methods of the God inspired teaching we find in scripture. "A little leaven leaveneth the whole lump" (Gal 5:9) and worldly methodology leads many to be deceived by errors that are routinely presented as truth, just as they have been deceived into believing 'John was the beloved disciple'.

For example, one of the case studies in the next book will touch on several errors that are taught about this key verse, "For God so loved the world, that he gave his only begotten Son, that whosoever believeth in him should not perish, but have everlasting life" (Fourth gospel 3:16). When this verse is quoted it is very common to hear some added comments like 'This is an example of God's unconditional love for you.' But it is hard to understand why any Bible student would allow that assertion to go unchallenged because it is obviously contrary to the plain text of the verse. To imply the verse was written to inform the readers thereof about an unconditional love for them is to twist the verse beyond recognition, since what the God-inspired writer wrote here is a conditional statement – and we see the condition explicitly stated in the verse "that whosoever believeth in him".

Should one conclude the blessing of "not perish, but have everlasting life" is applicable to all those who do <u>not</u> believe "in him"? Not according to the verse. Why not? Because the necessary condition was not met. Here we are not talking about whatever else scripture may say in other passages. We are talking about being faithful to accurately communicate what *this* verse says. This verse tells us the reason God "gave his only begotten Son" was **"that"** those who meet the condition ("believeth in him") should "not perish...", so the condition is vital to the verse. Therefore, it goes against the words of the verse to imply it was intended to inform everyone who reads or hears it about 'God's unconditional love' for them.

Because of this and other errors which are frequently taught about this well known verse, a case can be made that in our day it is literally the most misunderstood verse in the Bible and the next book in this series will present biblical evidence that will show why this is so. Yet as with the error on the beloved disciple, correcting a mistaken idea on a particular topic or verse is not as important as identifying the flaw in our thinking process that caused us to be deceived by the error. All of the books in this series will show how relying on God's word to "prove all things" can both correct our errors and improve our Bible study method. In Acts 24:16 Paul said, "I exercise myself, to have always a conscience void of offence toward God, and *toward* men" and the things we can do to follow his example include accurately communicating God's word and always striving to improve our understanding of it.

"A Fool Returneth to His Folly"

"As a dog returneth to his vomit, *so* a fool returneth to his folly" (Pr. 26:11). Those who see the biblical evidence herein will conclude it proves beyond a reasonable doubt John was not "the disciple whom Jesus loved" or they will conclude it did not do so. There is no third option. All who say they are still considering the evidence or will reserve judgment on the matter are refusing to state the obvious; they were **not** convinced by the data that was presented. When seeking the truth we can only judge based on the evidence we know about – and if that evidence is able to offer proof beyond a reasonable doubt then, by definition, it is unreasonable to refuse to side with that evidence.

One does not have to agree that scripture disproves the John idea. But by the same token, those who were not convinced by the biblical evidence that was offered are obliged to answer one question, Why not? Since the standard is <u>reasonable</u> doubt, a person who continues to believe the John tradition in spite of the biblical evidence would need to explain why it is reasonable to do so.

One can disagree with the conclusions of this book. However, if a person does so simply because he or she does not want to admit the John idea is a false teaching, then that is not reasonable doubt, it is sheer prejudice. Defenders of the John tradition may choose to believe non-Bible sources are more trustworthy than God's word on this matter. But if they do, then honesty demands they admit this is the reason for their disagreement.

Those who respect the authority of God's word and love the truth will certainly be willing to state why they believe scripture does or does not prove a given idea. Apart from any reasonable doubt, respect for God's word should move all who are aware of this biblical evidence to cease and desist promoting the false John tradition. As "scripture is profitable for correction" we should invite that correction on any issue, including the question of the authorship of the fourth gospel. Still, those who want to justify their decision to hang on to a false belief **after** they learn of biblical evidence to the contrary can always find a pretense for doing so. Nevertheless, scripture tells us, "a fool returneth to his folly". Conversely, "a wise *man* will hear, and will increase learning" (Pr. 1:5). Hearing the word of God and accepting the correction that it offers is thus declared to be the wise move. (Even on 'little' issues?)

"Thou shalt love the Lord thy God with all thy heart, and with all thy soul, and with all thy mind" (Mt. 22:37), said Jesus, leaving no wiggle room for those who might think they can ignore those parts of the Bible they do not like. This obliges us to also honor God with our words and be as accurate as we can be when discussing God's word. Therefore, those who know the biblical evidence proves John was not the author of the fourth gospel are obliged to stop referring to that book by the false title of *John*. While some may say it is okay to continue using that title for convenience or reference sake, what one cannot say is they use that title for God's sake because the title itself promotes the false idea that John was the author.

Jesus said, "To this end was I born, and for this cause came I into the world, that I should bear witness unto the truth" (Fourth gospel 18:37). Does this suggest he would agree the truth sometimes does not matter? If not, then we should strive to be **consistent** in our respect for truth and always seek to be accurate when we present God's word. Those who pay tribute to a false tradition, by continuing to promote it even after they are aware it is not biblical, are being inconsistent as far as respect for God's word is concerned. James 4:8, "Draw nigh to God, and he will draw nigh to you", is certainly a good reason to change when our beliefs and our ways are opposed to what scripture says. While some argue the importance of a given issue is what determines what 'matters', the fact is the authority of God's word is always the critical issue. This is true because apart from God's word one cannot even believe the foundation of the gospel which declares, "Christ died for our sins according to the scriptures; And that he was buried, and that he rose again the third day according to the scriptures" (1Cor. 15:3b-4).

"Every word of God *is* pure: he *is* a shield unto them that put their trust in him" (Pr. 30:5). If God's word is the foundation of our beliefs, then we have no reason to fear a closer inspection of the biblical evidence on any issue. Psalm 119 says, "Thy word *is* a lamp unto my feet, and a light unto my path". This and other verses make it clear the light of scripture is a blessing to the children of light, not a threat. Good information is the key to making a good decision. If you want good data look to God's word, "For the LORD giveth wisdom: out of his mouth *cometh* knowledge and understanding" (Pr. 2:6). So, if people try to turn you away from God's word by pointing you to some non-Bible source, including noted figures or an army of people who trust in tradition, remember "The fear of man bringeth a snare: but whoso putteth his trust in the LORD shall be safe" (Pr. 29:25). Let us obey the words of Jesus in Matthew 19:18, "Thou shalt not bear false witness".